EVERYTHING

PARENT'S GUIDE TO

RAISING YOUR ADOPTED CHILD

Dear Reader,

I've watched philosophies about adoption change dramatically over the forty years since I fought the child welfare system for the right to adopt two baby girls who were my foster daughters. I've actively worked with foster and adoptive families for many years, and ended up adopting three of my nine children. I also have an adopted brother and adopted grandchildren, as well as a dozen or so nieces, nephews, and cousins who are adopted.

This book is the result of years of experience and a great deal of research into the phenomenon of adoption as a significant, loving way to form a family. It is also an attempt by my editors and me to find the areas of truth (defined by behavioral research as well as anecdotal evidence) amidst all the rhetoric.

I would love to hear your story, to add it to the hundreds I've heard over the past year. Please contact me at Adams Media or on my Web site, *www.corrielynneplayer.com*, to share your ideas and thoughts about the special, joyous adventure of parenting through adoption.

Corrie Lynne Player

Welcome to

THE

EVERYTHING®

PARENT'S GUIDES

Everything® Parent's Guides are a part of the bestselling *Everything*® series and cover common parenting issues like childhood illnesses and tantrums, as well as medical conditions like asthma and juvenile diabetes. These family-friendly books are designed to be a one-stop guide for parents. If you want authoritative information on specific topics not fully covered in other books, *Everything*® Parent's Guides are your perfect solution.

 Alerts: Urgent warnings

 Essentials: Quick handy tips

 Facts: Important snippets of information

 Questions: Answers to common questions

PUBLISHER Karen Cooper

DIRECTOR OF ACQUISITIONS AND INNOVATION Paula Munier

MANAGING EDITOR, EVERYTHING SERIES Lisa Laing

COPY CHIEF Casey Ebert

ACQUISITIONS EDITOR Lisa Laing

SENIOR DEVELOPMENT EDITOR Brett Palana-Shanahan

EDITORIAL ASSISTANT Hillary Thompson

Visit the entire Everything® series at *www.everything.com*

THE EVERYTHING

PARENT'S GUIDE TO

RAISING YOUR ADOPTED CHILD

A complete handbook to welcoming your
adopted child into your heart and home

Corrie Lynne Player, M.Ed.
with Brette McWhorter Sember and Mary C. Owen, LCSW

Avon, Massachusetts

To my children, Dolly, Sherri, and Brian; my brother, Butchy; my grandson, Jaden; and my nephews, Jeremiah and Matt, who taught me just how special, unique, and strong families with adopted children can be.

• • •

An Everything® Series Book.
Everything® and everything.com® are registered trademarks of F+W Publications, Inc.

Published by Adams Media, an F+W Publications Company
57 Littlefield Street, Avon, MA 02322 U.S.A.
www.adamsmedia.com

ISBN 10: 1-59869-606-8
ISBN 13: 978-1-59869-606-6

Printed in Canada.

J I H G F E D C B A

Library of Congress Cataloging-in-Publication Data
is available from the publisher.

This book is available at quantity discounts for bulk purchases.
For information, please call 1-800-289-0963.

All the examples and dialogues used in this book are fictional, and have been created by the author to illustrate disciplinary situations.

▶**adoption** (a dop´ tion) n. **1.** Building a family through the process of concentrated, dedicated, enduring love, rather than biology.

Acknowledgments

Many wonderful people contributed to the shape and contents of this book: adoption organizations, professionals, and individuals from all three parts of the adoption triad. I want to especially thank the Adoption group on CafeMom and the many adoptees, birth parents, and adoptive parents who shared their stories, their challenges, and their suggestions. Most of all, I want to thank Dr. Karyn Purvis, an experienced educator, fellow author, and kind friend for her patience and help as I started the research necessary to produce this book.

Contents

Introduction

No other method of forming a family carries as many misconceptions, possibilities, and challenges as adoption. Most people who want to become parents just go ahead and let biology take its course. But when you decide to adopt, you must put up with a vast array of nosy people who investigate everything from your income to your parenting philosophy. And you quickly learn that all the good intentions in the world won't do you much good unless you have special training and support.

Generally, your adopted child is just like any other child—he needs food, shelter, kindness, loving discipline, and appropriate boundaries. Most of all, he needs a secure attachment to you and other members of your immediate family in order to develop physically and emotionally.

You may be just starting out on your adoption adventure. Perhaps you've found a birth mom on your own and are anxiously awaiting her due date or you're waiting for an international adoption to be approved so you can bring your child home. You may be involved in either a kinship or stepparent adoption. You could be enduring the long, complicated process of filling out forms, writing a dossier, and working with an agency. Perhaps you've endured infertility or child loss and are finally putting the pieces of your life together or feel a spiritual call to adopt, to give a home and future to a child from the foster care system or a third-world country. Maybe your child has been in your home for a while, and you need some friendly, sound advice from somebody who understands where you're coming from. This book will give you tips and direction and help you figure out where to go for more in-depth information, no matter what your situation is.

You will get important information about things like how to interact with birth parents and extended families, questions to ask yourself about whether or not you want to take on the challenges of older children, emotional pitfalls and unique discipline issues for adopted children, and how to provide the answers to hard questions like "Why didn't my birth mom keep me?"

Adoption is a wonderful way to form a family, but it's not for the thin of skin or faint of heart; it requires a strong sense of self and an almost mystical yearning to be a parent.

The Everything® Parent's Guide to Raising Your Adopted Child contains the latest research and opinions of adoption professionals, but it also gives advice from the real experts—adoptive parents, grown adoptees, and biological families. The descriptions and stories come from those who have adopted infants domestically, who have gone to Guatemala, Russia, China, and many other places around the world to adopt, or who have taken on older children, teens with special needs, or sibling groups. Please note that these stories are composites compiled from real situations, but with identifying information changed to protect the identities and privacy of those involved.

Let this book be your inspiration and your guide as you consider adoption and make important choices about a child that has joined or may join your family.

CHAPTER 1

Is Adoption Right for You?

Adoption may not be for everybody, but it may be for you. All adopted children, whether they come home from the hospital as newborns, are adopted from foster care, or come into your life from another country, have unique concerns that must be addressed. In most families, the special joys of adoption far outweigh the challenges.

Deciding to Adopt

Deciding whether or not to adopt is one of the most important choices you can make in your adult life. It's a choice that will ripple through your family, your community, and ultimately, society in general. You need to consider the options available to you and weigh them for yourself.

Considering How to Build a Family

You may be faced with a choice between assisted conception and adoption. Many families turn to adoption when they are unsuccessful conceiving or carrying a pregnancy to full term. Some parents know in their hearts they are meant to adopt children and never even consider pregnancy. Whatever path brings you to adoption, the decisions are yours alone, and in the eyes of adoption agencies, it is irrelevant what has brought you to consider adoption.

Choosing the Right Time

As you ponder your decision, you may ask, "When is the best time for me to adopt?" The answer will depend on your stage of life and your family's particular situation. If you have been yearning for a child for years and have no other children presently in the home, you may want to start the process as quickly as possible. If you already have small children, you should reflect on how soon the family will be able to adjust successfully to an additional family member.

It is important to consider the current needs of any existing children in your family; strong-willed children need closer supervision than more cooperative children. Many families with positive adoption outcomes report that they waited until their challenging children were old enough to be helpful before taking on a special needs infant or child.

If you have significant personal events going on in your life at the moment, consider the drain these changes have on your attention and energy. Adopted children, even infants, often need a longer adjustment period than biological children and might require changes in your work schedule or ability to return to work. You might find that right now is not an ideal time for you to adopt.

Financial Concerns and Considerations

Like many people, you may be under the impression that adopting a child always costs tens of thousands of dollars. The cost depends on which type of adoption you choose: private adoptions in which you support a birth mother through her pregnancy and delivery, and pay legal and agency fees, home-study costs, and so on can cost upward of $25,000; an international adoption may cost even more because of travel and bureaucratic complications. Adopting a child from a public agency (foster care) is much less expensive in initial costs.

Some states offer forms of financial help, and you may qualify for programs such as:

- African American Adoptions Online
- Christian World Adoptions

- Building Families Fund
- Employer adoption expense reimbursement programs
- State payments to help care for a special needs child you adopt
- Federal adoption tax credits

If you are involved in a kinship adoption (adopting a child who is a relative, see Chapter 2 for more information), you may only need to cover simple legal fees or may qualify for assistance from states who want to keep your relative's child out of the foster care system.

 Fact

Want more information on where to find financial help for adoption? If you type "Financial Resources for Adoption" into your Internet search engine, more than two million possibilities will pop up. An example is Tomorrow Is a Gift.com, which will give you twenty-two pages of resources to consider.

Keep in mind that actually raising your adopted child will cost whatever it would have cost if she had been born to you. It's important to understand the financial impact a child will have on your family. Most families find that the joy a child brings is worth much more than the money it costs to raise her. Adopted children can have emotional difficulties that require special services. Whatever the reason, it is important to understand that providing the necessary services to address the emotional problems can make significant demands on a family's finances.

Foster Care as an Inexpensive Option

If you don't have a lot of money, yet have a strong desire to give a child a permanent family, you can go through the licensing process to become a foster adopt home. Foster parents are paid monthly stipends to help cover some of the cost of caring for foster children. Being a foster parent means you must accept that the children who come into your home may not stay, and may eventually be reunited with their parents or relative. Every year, tens of thousands of children cycle into the foster care system, with 500,000 remaining in foster care. Many of these children are adopted, and as the foster parent, you are in a good position to adopt the child you have fostered.

Finding the Right Adoption Experience for You

If you have decided that you have the capacity necessary to be a successful adoptive parent, you must consider the types of adoptions available to you. Adoption today is far different from even a decade ago, and you have many options and possibilities. For example, thousands of older and or disabled children wait in foster care for families to step forward and give them permanent homes; there are children of every race and gender being placed through private and public agencies; and some birth mothers are looking to place their babies independent of agencies.

When considering all the adoption options, you need to consider your comfort level with each one. Would you be happy adopting a child from foster care who had to be removed from her parents due to abuse? How would you feel raising a child from another country who obviously looks nothing like you? How comfortable would you be having a birth mother who wants ongoing contact with the child? Are you nervous working with a birth mother without an agency involved? You must educate yourself about the details of each type of adoption and ask yourself these kinds of questions as you evaluate your options and consider what will work best for your family.

Though adoption options will be discussed in depth throughout this book, the following is a brief overview of the available avenues for adoption.

Private Agency Adoption

If you want to adopt a baby, this is one common pathway. You first find an adoption agency that then screens you and matches you with a birth mother. The birth mother may or may not participate in the placement decision. The baby comes home to you from the hospital. However, keep in mind that it can take many months or even a year or longer to be matched to a birth mother.

Public Agency Adoption

This is adoption from foster care. If you do not wish to adopt an infant, foster care may be for you. There are many children of every age waiting to be placed in a home after their parents' rights have been terminated or surrendered. You can adopt groups of siblings or just one child of any age you choose. There are also many children with special needs in foster care waiting for a family. Public agency adoptions are generally very fast.

You might also consider accepting an at-risk placement. This means you become a foster parent and accept a child who has not yet been freed for adoption. The termination of the birth parents' rights is in progress, but not definite. This allows you to bring a child into your home immediately, but you must accept the uncertainty of the situation. Some prospective adoptive parents find this very stressful emotionally, especially if the child is removed from the home after he has become attached to family members.

International Adoption

There are many children available for adoption from orphanages and agencies in other countries. These children are not usually available until they are older babies or toddlers. The list of countries that permit international adoption changes frequently, so you need to work with an agency that knows the laws and can help you find a child. Each country has its own requirements. In almost all international adoptions, you will need to travel to the country once or twice before finalization of the adoption. You will need help cutting through the red tape in your child's country of origin, and your agency will provide you with a translator and or a guide. This type of adoption can take up to a year to complete.

Independent Adoption

If you locate a birth mother yourself, you can adopt her child. You will need an attorney to handle the paperwork. Some people ask an agency to help process the adoption as well. This is another way to adopt an infant. Finding a baby yourself can take a long time and involve a lot of heartbreak if the birth mother changes her mind.

Assess Your Emotional and Physical Status

Adoption is best entered into after a lot of thought and research. Deciding to adopt depends on myriad questions, most of which can only be answered by you and your spouse or partner. You must first determine that you are ready and able to cope with the adoption both emotionally and physically; raising a child requires all of you.

Deal with Your Emotional Issues First

Your self-examination should include recognition of semiconscious or subconscious emotions. If you've been trying to conceive for years or have been told that your infertility is irreversible, you need to grieve over the child that might have been, as well as any pregnancy losses you suffered. It is important to understand that grief can be a complex combination of anger, sadness, and fear. Many people find it necessary to receive professional help in their grieving process to fully resolve their feelings and be emotionally available for an adopted child. Your newly adopted child will need to have his own special place in your heart and shouldn't be seen as a substitute.

Consider Your Family's Emotional Health

Children deserve to be brought into a strong, successful marriage or a stable single-parent home. If your home life is currently in conflict or if you feel insecure about the future, now is not the best time to consider adoption. Certainly don't think of a new child as a way to fix a problem in your marriage.

Be sure that you and your spouse are in agreement about the adoption. A main reason for failed or dysfunctional adoptions is a lack of agreement between the parents. You must present a united front and be prepared to begin this journey together, ready to enjoy whatever it brings you and willing to address difficulties proactively.

Alert!

If you already have a biological child and want to add to your family through adoption, be sure that you understand that your new child cannot be viewed solely as a companion and playmate for your current child. Don't let your current child's desire for a sibling be the main reason for adopting. Take into consideration the impact a new child will have on everybody in the family.

Be sure your immediate family is 100 percent in favor of adopting, because even one dissenter can sabotage the relationship. For example, the Nelson family had three children, a four-year-old boy, an eight-year-old girl, and a thirteen-year-old boy, when they decided to adopt their fourteen-year-old niece, Melinda, whose parents had lost their rights. Although Melinda had lived with them for most of two years, Sam, the thirteen year old, didn't like his cousin; he resented her taking over the eldest spot in the family, among other things. After the adoption, serious problems erupted and Melinda eventually went into foster care. Family and individual counseling, before making the adoption commitment, might have resolved issues and saved the family the tragedy of a failed adoption.

Adoption is a relationship that can create strong emotional intensity. It can be even more complex than marriage because one of the parties is a dependent child who often feels powerless and vulnerable. Being sensitive to the wide range of possible emotions that all family members may experience in the adoption process is essential. Remember that adoption is forever and should be entered into not only with optimism, but with a strong commitment to addressing the needs of all family members.

Consider Physical Limitations

If you, your spouse, or one of your children is dealing with a serious illness, chronic condition, or other physical limitation, you need to consider how able you are to care for a new child. Parenting is a very physical job—lifting and carrying are integral parts in the first few years. People with physical limitations can most definitely be successful adoptive parents, but it is always best to consider how a new child will affect you and your family.

Assess Your Lifestyle

Your career, residence, and obligations to your family are important factors when you are considering adoption. The emotional age of your adopted child will dictate just how much time you can spend away from home, as will the availability of reliable child care. If you adopt a child with attachment disturbance, behavioral problems, or disabilities, your career (or your partner's) may have to take second place. Some children who have lost or never had safe, caring families may need time, sometimes years, to attach to their adoptive parents. You can't solve behavioral problems when you are away from your child, and a child with a physical disability needs involved, consistent care.

If you have obligations to extended family, those obligations can impact whether a particular child will mesh well with your family. For example, an aged parent who lives with you may divert too much energy for you to be able to give an infant or special-needs child sufficient attention. In the same situation, however, an older child or teen may become a support and comfort to her grandparent and you, freeing you up to be able to meet everyone's needs. However, due to early childhood stressors, an older adopted child may not be able to meet the typical expectations of responsibility or empathic understanding that parents would normally have of a child of that age.

Understanding Adoption

Before you can make a decision about adoption, you have to understand how it works and what kind of impact it has on everyone involved. Adoption takes a child from one family unit and permanently places him in another. Everyone involved is impacted by this major move, and understanding some of the effects can help you make an educated decision. Adoption is sometimes referred to as a triad—a three-sided figure made up of the birth parents, adoptive parents, and the child. All three are interrelated and linked to each other. Even if your child never knew his birth parents, the triad still exists and is an important part of life for all of you.

Legal Process

In every adoption, there must be a legal proceeding that frees the child for adoption—that breaks the legal bond between the child and the birth parents. When birth parents place a child for adoption, they must provide legal consent to the adoption by appearing before a court or signing a paper giving up their rights to the child. When a child is removed from a home by the state and freed for an adoption, the court severs the legal bond between child and birth parents, making the child eligible for adoption. In international adoptions, children are placed for adoption, or are sometimes left at orphanages, with the birth parent essentially consenting to the adoption.

The Impact of Early Experiences

When deciding if you could be a good adoptive parent, you should be aware of how adoption can affect a child. Raising an adoptive child is like raising a biological child most of the time; the child will be yours and part of your family. You will love him as much as any natural child, and you will face ups and downs together.

However, some of the challenges you will encounter with your adopted child will relate directly to his adoption.

 Essential

All children need nourishing food, clean, safe surroundings, and unconditional, persistent love. Your adoptive child will have these same needs, but may also require help to overcome the lack of proper care before and after he was born, depending on the situation he was in. You must ponder your fitness for parenting a child whose earliest experiences could have a lingering and sometimes profound effect.

Even if your child is placed in your arms within days of his birth and received good prenatal care, he will eventually begin to wonder about his biological origins. His early years won't be much different from any child's, but by the time he enters school, being adopted may become an issue. No matter how much love he receives from you, he will wonder about where he came from and question why he's with you. You must be ready to answer his questions in a way that reassures him about your abiding, enduring commitment (see Chapter 15).

Reasons Your Prospective Child Needs a New Family

The child you adopt may have been given up by a healthy mother who decided she couldn't parent, or may have been removed from a dysfunctional, dangerous home by the state; he may have been abandoned, or been placed in an overseas orphanage by parents overwhelmed by poverty. Each child has his own history; your role is to provide a new home for the child and help him eventually understand, in the best possible light, the choices made by the birth parents that led to the adoption.

Children who become adoptable are in the situation involuntarily. Some children of toddler age and older may feel powerless and hopeless if they've changed homes more than once through foster care. Infants have an innate desire to be with an attachment figure, a parent who will consistently meet their needs and assure their survival. Children whose birth parents, their attachment figures, have disappeared have to deal with that loss. Even children who had no contact with their birth parents will still wonder about them. Through adoption, you can give your child a loving home and begin what some mental health professionals call "The Dance of Attachment"—a process through which your child becomes deeply attached to you, a trustworthy parent, and you have bonded to your child—which will bring you great rewards.

 *Question?*

How can I find reliable information about adoption that will help me make a decision?
The Internet is a great tool, but it isn't selective—anybody can put information up for public consumption, and some of that information may be distorted or false. Instead of just searching the word "adoption," go to reputable sites like the American Academy of Pediatrics (*www.AAP.org*), The National Council for Adoption (*www.adoptioncouncil.org*), or Adoptive Families (*www.adoptivefamilies.org*).

Attitudes about Adoption

As you ponder whether or not you'd be a good adoptive parent, you'll encounter diverse opinions, ranging from those who believe that only biological relatives should be able to adopt, to those who believe that adoptive families are superior to biological families. Complicating the picture is a public perception that adoption is somehow inferior to forming a family through giving birth. The rhetoric on both sides tends to be hard to follow, but you can sort out fact from fiction by studying the results of scientific research, talking to experienced parents and adult adoptees, and most of all, listening to your own instincts; only you can make the decision that is best for your family.

Adoption Has Become More Accessible

Only a generation ago, adoption wasn't very common. The ones that did take place were closed (secretive) and rarely occurred across racial lines. Few people understood the psychological implications of adoption, but then governments began to address child welfare issues and the social sciences became well-known professions, with thousands choosing to focus on adoption issues, especially attachment and bonding.

Removing Social Barriers to Adoption

Two groundbreaking books helped change public perception about adoption. In 1954, Helen Doss detailed her adoption of nearly a dozen minority and mixed-race children in her book, *The Family Nobody Wanted.* She described how she learned that race made no difference in the personalities and growth of her children. She also discussed her efforts to armor them against the ingrained racism of the time. Jean Paton's book, *The Adopted Break Silence,* described forty adults, adopted as children, who shared their stories about the need to have connections to "all the pieces" of their lives. Thirty of the forty participants described their adoptions as "wonderful" or "generally positive," but even those who were most satisfied felt that adults should have access to their original birth information.

In the early '70s, therapists and mental health workers began to promote the importance of a psychological parent (a person the child emotionally identifies as a parent in her life) rather than a biological parent, and advocated the necessity of speed in placing children into permanent families.

More legislation was passed to address problems with the struggle between parental rights and child advocacy in foster care and state agency adoption placements. The 1980 Adoption Assistance and Child Welfare Act encouraged states to act on the findings of psychologists and therapists for quick, lasting placements. The Adoption and Safe Families Act, passed in 1997, stressed "permanency planning" and "represented a policy shift away from family reunification and toward adoption."

 Fact

In 1955, Bertha and Harry Holt adopted eight Korean War orphans, which required a special act of Congress. They went on to establish the Holt Adoption Agency, which set the standard for adoptions, both local and international, and is a major agency today.

All of these movements and laws together have resulted in adoption becoming a process that is not only well accepted by society, but one that is easier than ever. Children no longer have to wait years in foster homes for birth parents who they will never be reunited with, and international adoption is now common.

Government Intervention

Unlike a few years ago, adoptive parents today are no longer restricted by race, nationality, marital status, or sexual orientation from becoming a parent. There's a huge national effort to bring adoptable children to the attention of prospective parents, regardless of their race. However, even though Congress now forbids race from being used as the sole criterion for adoption placement decisions (1994), same-race placement is still considered an important guideline by many agencies and social service departments.

Alert!

The media has contributed to public awareness about the plight of older adoptable children through Oklahoma's Wednesday's Child, Pennsylvania's Friday's Child, and California's Waiting Child programs. Hundreds of children across the country have found homes because of such programs.

The Multiethnic Placement Act prohibited agencies receiving federal funds from denying transracial adoptions on the sole basis of race, but permitted the use of race as one factor. In 1996, the Inter-Ethnic Adoption Amendment made it impermissible to employ race at all.

Additionally, private agencies such as Casey Family Services, the North American Council on Adoptable Children, Great Kids, Inc., We Care Child & Family Services, and Adoption Ark coordinate with government agencies to help meet the needs of tens of thousands of children who wait in foster care.

CHAPTER 2

Growing Areas of Adoption

There are far more roads to adoption than ever before, and more nontraditional adoptions are taking place. Today, you can adopt your stepchild, grandchild, or other family members. Single and older parents and same-sex couples, who in the past may have been discriminated against, are now some of the more prominent adopters. Hundreds of thousands of children in the United States and millions of children around the world need families, and adoption agencies are looking for new avenues to place these children.

Adoption by Grandparents or Extended Family

If you adopt a grandchild, niece, nephew, or cousin, you will join one of the fastest growing areas of adoption: kinship placements. Because the parent, a relative, passes away or can no longer parent her own child, you may find yourself adding a child to your family. Courts and agencies like kinship adoptions because they allow the child to remain within the same extended family. Usually, a child does not have to start over with strangers when he continues within the same family.

Benefits of Being a Kinship Parent

If you are a grandparent or an older relative adopting, you may welcome the chance to "use thirty years of accumulated wisdom," as one grandfather commented at the hearing that gave him permanent custody of his four-year-old granddaughter and her six-year-old brother.

You may be content with where you are in life, but find that the adoption presents you with the opportunity to make a huge difference in the life of an extended family member. You can do so with some training and professional support.

One couple, Sue Lee and Roger, took in Sue Lee's cousin, Lucy, whose mother had died of complications of anorexia and drug abuse, and who had been abusive toward Lucy. "I had no idea it would be so hard," said Sue Lee after the eight-year-old was dropped off at their house. "Here was this cute red-headed girl. She looked like an angel, but within two weeks reality set in." Sue Lee described her shock at discovering that Lucy would erupt into volcanic bursts of anger, almost without provocation or warning. At other times, she would withdraw into herself, hiding in the closet and hoarding food under her pillow.

 Essential

Grandparents as Parents (GAP) is a national support group based in California formed to help grandparents deal with the issues of parenting when their grown children cannot. Their Web site, *www.grandparentsasparents.com*, contains useful information and tips for forming local groups.

They consulted with their pediatrician, who had recently completed training for meeting the special needs of neglected children. He was able to offer specific advice for dealing with certain behaviors, including dietary changes and activities that directly impacted Lucy's brain chemistry. He also prescribed medications to replace missing chemicals that he believed drove her anger. His treatments, combined with patience and her parents' loving reassurances, gradually turned Lucy into the smiling young adult she is today. Although most adoptive children do not need medication, it's important to understand that there are resources available to you should you find yourself having to manage an adopted child's unstable emotional behaviors.

Moving Out of Your Comfort Zone

If you have older children, you may have breathed a sigh of relief when your youngest started school, and looked forward to devoting more time to your career. You may have already retired or be close to it and anxious to enjoy a calmer lifestyle. However, unexpected events in your family may force you to reexamine your priorities.

The adoption may create a big change in your life. You may need to make changes to your:

- Income
- Career
- Living arrangements
- Social life
- Travel plans
- Schedule
- Future plans
- Relationships

It can be hard to reprioritize when you are older, but doing so makes a big difference in the life of the child you are adopting.

Older Siblings Adopting Younger Siblings

Sometimes, the unexpected loss of parents leads to a situation in which older siblings adopt younger siblings. Anecdotal evidence from private and public agencies indicates that siblings can and do successfully parent younger brothers and sisters. However, you must meet certain conditions that have to do with whether or not you can be a parent with all of the responsibilities that entails. Being a parent requires physical stability and emotional maturity. Taking on the responsibility of parenting younger siblings at a time when you are also grieving the loss of a parent or parents can be overwhelming. Many times, an older sibling finds he can be most supportive to younger siblings by remaining involved in their lives without taking on the parent role.

Lifestyle Requirements

The most important condition to adopting a sibling is that you are at a stable place in your life. You should have completed your own education (or at least be self-supporting if you are in school) and be a functional adult, capable of parenting. You must have a permanent residence and an income sufficient to provide for your sibling, and you must be able to demonstrate that stability in a court of law. The exact requirements vary from state to state, so be sure you have good legal advice from an attorney who specializes in adoption and custody cases.

 Essential

Visit the American Bar Association online at *www.abanet.org*. At the top of the page, you will see a "search" block, right under the site's name. Fill in the word "adoption." You will then be taken to links for all states, where you can further refine your search for adoption laws and requirements.

Emotional Requirements

You must be able to model appropriate relationships and social behaviors. The court will look closely at your living situation to be sure it's stable. They look more favorably on married couples than those who are cohabitating (although cohabitation is not a bar to adopting, it is simply a factor the court will consider). Single siblings can also adopt, provided their lives are settled.

In addition, as with any adoption, the court will research your background to check for any arrest warrants or legal entanglements. They may examine your employment records for long-term jobs to decide whether or not you have sufficient financial resources.

Another condition is that the age difference between you and your sibling be approximately ten years. Being a parent is very different from being a friend or sibling, and it involves maturity that usually comes from age. Making the mental shift from siblings to parent-child is very difficult. You need to establish your authority and get your sibling to accept it. This can be hard to do, but when you and your sibling only have each other, you will probably start with a high motivation to find a way to make it work.

 ***Fact***

Adoptions by siblings closer in age than the usual ten years have occurred, because it often makes more sense to place a child with a sibling with whom she already has a relationship than with an unknown family member.

Finally, the social worker or court will probe you with what-if questions that will reveal your intellectual and emotional capacity to make moral and disciplinary decisions, and to follow through on those decisions. You will be asked such questions as:

- How will you motivate your sibling to stay in school?
- What sort of supervision will you provide while you're at work?
- If your sibling defies you, how will you respond?
- What will you do if your friends want you to go out to a bar but you don't have a sitter?
- What would you do if your sibling was using drugs?
- What kind of discipline will you use?

These kinds of questions are designed to determine your maturity and parenting capabilities. Think about as many scenarios as you can, write them down, then write down your possible answers.

Adoption by Stepparents

If you're a stepparent, many aspects of the adoption will be different from other forms because of the biological connection the child has to your spouse. Some states offer streamlined adoption processes for stepparents. Once you adopt, you'll no longer be the stepparent, you'll be the legal parent in every sense of the word. This distinction is crucial, because your family will no longer be blended, it will be primary. However, you will still deal with semantics, because your child will be aware of the biological parent.

Alert!

When there's an adoption, the biological parent has no legal right to see or spend time with the child. In some open or kinship adoptions, visitation with biological parents is agreed on without the force of law. In some states, these agreements are contained in the adoption decree, yet are generally not very enforceable. Unless you sign some sort of contract for visitation, you don't have to let anyone visit or contact your child.

The age of the child at the time of the adoption is also important. When children who are adopted by stepparents are infants or are very young, they won't have the same conflicted feelings an older child or teen might have. You are the parent, and the law backs you in making decisions for your child, but you should take into consideration existing relationships. Although you have become the legal parent, the biological parent still may be important to your child; you can't undo the emotional bonds that exist. See Chapter 13 for further discussion.

Continued Contact for Biological Family

As a stepparent who is adopting, you should respect the child's needs and the emotional welfare of the whole family. There are probably family members on the biological father's or mother's side (whoever is giving up parenting rights) who don't want to lose contact with the child, such as aunts, uncles, and grandparents.

Also, when a parent whose rights have been terminated remarries and has other children, the issue of half-siblings arises. Your child may want to have a relationship with those siblings.

Your primary consideration in all this must be your child's emotional well-being. If he has loving, close relationships with extended family, he will reap great benefits as he grows up. However, some children experience complicated grief over adoption when they have repeated contact with biological family members; sometimes the contact causes more longing and unresolved feelings about their loss.

Emotional Ramifications for the Child

The emotional rewards of being adopted by a stepparent can be enormous for the child involved, depending on his age. He may feel a sense of loss or have concerns about his birth parent as he grows up. Typically, feelings about adoption and the biological family change when a child moves into different developmental stages. It is important as an adoptive parent to be willing to revisit adoption issues and process them with your child in developmentally appropriate ways.

A child who is adopted due to a parent relinquishing rights may require counseling to deal with lingering feelings of abandonment or rejection. Be sensitive and supportive; help your child understand that what the other parent did was out of concern for what would be best in the long run.

Help your stepchild feel special about his adoption by frequently expressing your love and the choice you made. You weren't forced into adopting him, it was something you very much wanted to do. When the adoption is finalized, you may choose to give your child a lasting gift such as a watch with something commemorative engraved on it. Mark the anniversary every year by going out to dinner or a movie and buying a small gift, such as a toy or game. Predictable rituals repeated through the years can help children accept an adoption.

 Essential

Try to make certain that relatives don't play favorites among your children, favoring those related to them by blood over those related through marriage and adoption. Any significant distinctions between siblings, whether they're biological, step, or adopted, can be toxic to your family's emotional well-being.

Adoption by Single Parents

According to the latest census data, single-parent homes with children under eighteen make up almost 50 percent of all households in the United States. And more and more single people are choosing to adopt. While in the past some adoption agencies have been wary of single parents, they have come to realize that what's important is not the number of parents a child has, but the quality of parenting.

Ramifications for Single-Parent Households

While agencies in the past have been cautious about accepting single-parent adoption, attitudes are changing, and the sheer number of children needing permanent homes, combined with the flood of interest from single adults, has brought about major changes.

Your greatest challenge may come when you realize the job you're considering is one that's difficult even when two people share it! Parenting solo can be a lonely, frustrating duty, but as most of those who've gone before you will attest, it can also be where you will find your greatest joy.

You might find yourself in a situation like Kara. Kara was a teacher in her late thirties who was worried that she would never find the right man in time to have a family, so she decided to adopt. She adopted a beautiful little girl from Russia she named Emma. Kara relied on her parents and sister as resources: Her parents often took Emma for a weekend to give Kara some free time; and her sister was always available at the drop of a hat to babysit. Kara's friends welcomed Emma into their circle and encouraged their own children to make friends with her. Kara found that being a parent was more challenging than she ever imagined, but the joy that Emma brought to her life more than made up for it.

Alert!

Single parents need an effective support system. Be sure to have a neighbor or two, as well as a few family members, to assist with child care. No one can do it alone! Backup is important for planning nights out and for help when your child is home sick from school. It's also important emotionally—you need to know there are people you can rely on and talk to when the going gets tough.

Resources are available to help ease the burden of being the sole breadwinner and disciplinarian and main child-care provider. Start by accessing *www.parentswithoutpartners.org*. They have local chapter meetings that can be very helpful to single parents just getting started. Then ask around at your child's school or day care; you can also ask the principal or director to give your phone number to any single parents he thinks might be willing to share stories and advice.

Overcoming the Challenges of Single Parenting

Having the sole responsibility as a parent can seem overwhelming at times. Don't try to do everything yourself—reach out to family and friends and be sure you have a support system that extends beyond your day care. You need a long-term person, such as an extended family member, who will support you in your parenting role. Continuity and stability are essential, so look for someone who's stable enough to be there for you over time.

Adoption by Older Parents

People in America live much longer than they did 100 years ago. Many have two and even three careers, and they also often have two families, raising one, and when those children are grown, having another.

If you are past the age of being able to biologically have more children or easily keep up with young children, you can still parent by adopting a child or sibling group. In fact, you are part of a demographic community that could solve the problem of not enough stable-family homes for older children, teens, and young adults who have aged out of foster care. Most countries that permit international adoptions have age limits, so international adoption may not be an option for you. If you seek to adopt through a birth mother or private agency, you may also find that age is a problem. However, there is no age limit for public agency adoptions.

Advantages of Parenting over Fifty

As an older parent, you are probably more secure in your career and personal life. Financial problems don't figure as prominently as they may for younger people. With your greater experience, you may also be more adept at handling conflicts and maintaining discipline.

Jossette and Manuel, in their early fifties, decided to become foster parents. They wanted to help children using what they'd learned, and really weren't interested in starting another family. But when a sibling group of eight- and ten-year-old girls and a twelve-year-old boy was placed with them and freed for adoption, they changed their minds. They decided the three children needed a family much more than they needed to enjoy an empty nest. Now they plan to adopt their seventeen-year-old foster child, who would age out of the system within a year and had no parents or extended family.

Like Jossette and Manuel, you may be in a position to add to your family through foster care adoption. Even if you're in your sixties, adoption of a teenager or young adult could add depth to your life, and heal a very real hole in the heart of a young person who can then become a contributing member of society because of your support.

Special Considerations for Older Parents

Some of the drawbacks of adopting as an older parent are health and energy issues. Martha, a fifty-two-year-old nurse, adopted a disabled four-year-old boy who had been abandoned at the hospital where she worked. Martha admits that her heart made the decision, and she didn't think through just how time consuming and exhausting caring for a young child would be at her age, especially as a single parent. She says now, "If I'd known how hard this was going to be, I might not have done it. But, now that Tracy is grown and living happily in a group home, I have all the joy of being his mom and I know that I made a significant difference in his life."

Other drawbacks might include pressure from your adult children, who may see the adoption as not only taking time and energy away from them, but also diluting their inheritance. This can be a sensitive situation, because it can drive a wedge between you and your children, and possibly with your grandchildren as well. You should assess your relationships with your grown children and figure out how to communicate your reasons for adopting to them. Also, consider that you have the right to pursue adoption whether or not your adult children agree.

Adoption by Same-Sex Couples

Although a March 2007 report compiled by the Urban Institute and the Williams Institute at University of California at Los Angeles School of Law stated that 65,000 adopted children are being raised by same-sex parents in the United States, adoption by gay and lesbian couples is still contested in some states.

According to an Urban Institute report, laws in most states don't specifically ban adoption by same-sex couples. Washington D.C. and eleven states have decreed that sexual orientation cannot be a factor in adoptions by same-sex couples. Currently, three states do deny the rights of gays and lesbians to adopt, though only one does so explicitly.

In Mississippi, single gays and lesbians can adopt; however, same-sex couples cannot. Utah has a statute barring unmarried couples from adopting or becoming foster parents. Florida is the only state that specifically bans homosexuals from adopting, though they do allow them to become foster parents.

Many people oppose the idea of families headed by a same-sex couple for religious reasons, while others disagree and feel that many children awaiting adoption would benefit from opening adoption to same-sex couples and increasing the number of potential adopting families. Public opinion about the issue is almost evenly split among Americans. In a March 2006 Pew Research Center poll, 46 percent of Americans support gay and lesbian adoption, which is a rise from 38 percent in 1999. This shift may have an influence in adoption policy in coming years, and prospective adoptive parents and interested parties should keep apprised of proposed changes in their state's legislation.

There are many sources of information regarding same-sex adoption, including Web sites and books, some of which can be found in the Appendices at the end of this book.

CHAPTER 3

Preparing for Adoption

Once you've decided you want to adopt, you're probably anxious to get started, but you should begin to make emotional, financial, and material preparations before you are matched with a child. These preparations will ensure your adoption adventure is a rewarding experience for you, your family, and the child you will raise to independent adulthood. The process is complicated because it involves so many variables, many of which are hard to predict. This unpredictability means you must deal with emotional highs and lows, subject yourself to scrutiny, and above all, put your potential child's needs first.

Prepare Yourself and Your Family Emotionally

You'll need to be flexible and have huge amounts of patience as you navigate the adoption maze. Sometimes you'll wait months or, more realistically, years before you receive a child in your home or the adoption becomes final. Adoption is doubly hard because not only are you dealing with the vagaries of the human heart, you are dealing with red tape and bureaucracy.

You'll also need courage and a strong sense of self. Be confident in your personal choices and your reasons for wanting to adopt so you can meet your family's needs and, if necessary, deal with disappointment if an adoption falls through or placement takes longer than you hoped.

Find the Help You Need

The adoption process can be extremely frustrating, and you'll need to roll with the punches that may come. Taking proactive steps to enrich your life and improve your skills will help make your experience more rewarding and less draining. Start by trying to put together a large, supportive network.

One of the most important resources you can have is an extended family who will back up your decision. Having your family on board with the adoption will enhance your emotional stability. If you don't have enough family resources, actively seek friends who will encourage and lift you. Seek the company of people who will offer you non-judgmental support.

 *Alert!*

Adoption will take a lot out of you emotionally. The hardest part can be the waiting—waiting for placement, and then the steps to finalize it. You have to reconcile yourself to the fact that waiting is a normal part of the process. You'll worry about things going wrong; everyone worries about this, but most adoptions have no problems.

Surround yourself with as many supportive people as possible. If your family and or friends can't be supportive of your adoption decision and there's a risk of them becoming a negative influence, you may be forced to limit contact with them or make the subject of the adoption off limits. At the very least, ask that they support you, even if they cannot support your choice.

Helping Family and Friends Understand

Try to be patient with anyone who means a lot to you who is not completely on board with your decision to adopt. They have not been beside you as you read, pondered, and discussed the pros and cons of bringing a child unrelated by blood into your family. You may occasionally get fed up or wish you could, as one adoptive dad said, "Open my grandma's head and stuff in all the good things I've learned."

An adoptive mom who endured years of infertility before adopting said after she adopted that she was able to educate the important people in her life. She helped them see that she loved her adopted child just as much as any mother loves her biological child.

 Essential

> With all the nature versus nurture debates going on, you might start feeling insecure. Genetic and biological aspects can have a powerful impact on a child's temperament and capabilities; however, fully embracing your adopted child into your family will make her just as much a "real" family member as any biological child. You didn't carry your child in your body, but your heart (and hers) understands that you're her "real" parent.

If you just don't think you can come up with the words that will explain how you feel, try giving family members a book like *From God's Arms to My Arms to Yours* by Michael McLean or *Two Little Girls: A Memoir of Adoption* by Theresa Reid, a well-written, powerful book about international adoption.

Preparing Existing Children

Bringing a new child into an existing family through adoption is different than bringing one in through birth. Most children experience sibling rivalry and jealousy because it's perfectly normal to want to be the center of attention. Preparing for the adoption should involve you and your children holding in-depth discussions and exploring feelings and issues. Read books to your younger children about adoption. If you are adopting internationally, familiarize yourself and your children with information about that country or culture. Read books about adoption and child care and take classes offered by your agency and or local mental health associations.

Strategies for Reassuring Children

Your children need to know, on a fundamental level, that love expands to fill the family, it doesn't divide. In other words, just because you have four children doesn't mean each child only has 25 percent of your love. You need to find a way to make sure that each child feels a love that is constant and essential.

Remember that time and attention are as important to children as food and water. Before and after the new child arrives, be sure to find individual time for your child. Use your imagination to help your child feel your love:

- Set aside special times to read a story, play an interactive game, or just cuddle.
- Ask questions about school, play dates, and other activities where you may be apart.
- Look into his eyes and say, "I love you" at least once a day.
- Leave love notes on his pillow or in his lunch box.
- Pray together or share inspirational thoughts.

Waiting rooms at doctors' or dentists' offices or time alone in the car are good opportunities for family interactions. But experts agree that meal times are by far the most important and effective means for enhancing family ties; make the effort to sit down together several times a week, or every day if possible.

Meeting the Legal Requirements of Adoption

There are several steps you must complete in order to be approved to adopt. They include a home study, writing a dossier, going through a background check, and assembling all the paperwork you need to present to the judge who will finalize the adoption.

 Fact

> Public and private adoption agencies have their own internal idiosyncrasies—all of which are supervised by the state where their offices are located. You can find a great deal of information about state laws by accessing *www.childwelfare.gov*, the Web site for the Child Welfare Information Gateway, sponsored by the U.S. Department of Health and Human Services, Administration for Children, Youth, and Families.

Be aware that the U.S. federal government and each of the fifty states have their own laws and regulations governing the adoptive relationship, and foreign countries are even more complicated. Therefore, the required forms will vary considerably, but there are certain general prerequisites, described below.

Background Check

This document is required by every state and country; it is designed to ensure that you are who you say you are. A background check usually requires you to go to your local police department for fingerprinting and to fill out a Background Screening Application. The BSA requires a photocopy of your driver's license and or passport. A criminal records check will be run as well. If you have lived in your resident state less than three years, on average, you may also be asked for a clearance from your previous state. A fee is normally charged for these checks. Things will get more complicated if you were born outside of the United States or lived abroad more than sixty days in any calendar year. In that case, you'll have to rely on your agency or an adoption attorney to direct you.

Dossier or Personal Biography

This autobiography will help your agency understand who you are and which child would best suit you. Try to enjoy writing this very important document, because it can give you great insight into yourself and your motivations. Describe your childhood, where you lived, your relationship with your parents, and people who influenced the direction of your life. You should also be specific about your parenting philosophy and what you feel you would offer a child. Photos from your childhood, as well as your life right now, should illustrate what's important to you. These can be very effective in gaining the attention of those who will decide which child will be yours.

 Essential

If you are planning to adopt a baby from a birth mother or private agency, you will probably also need to write a Dear Birth Mother Letter, which is a shorter version of your biography. Some parents also put together scrapbooks for the birth mother to look through. None of these are legal requirements, but if you are searching for a birth mother to pick you, they might be worthwhile.

You will likely have to attach a birth certificate and a marriage certificate, if applicable. You will need to include information about your salary, job, friends, religion, activities, and hobbies.

The dossier also contains letters of reference from acquaintances, business associates, clergy, and others. In addition, you will have to provide a medical form signed by a licensed physician that attests to your physical and mental health.

Home Study

This study is done by a social worker who visits your home and summarizes information from your biography. It helps your agency visualize the place where you live, determine if it's suitable for a child of a particular age, and determine if you are able to care for a child.

You will have at least two interviews with the social worker conducting the study. The first interview usually takes place in the social worker's office and the second in your home. Among other things, your social worker will require a floor plan of your home, an emergency exit strategy, and a safety inspection.

Adoption agencies look for your home to be clean and safe. Exactly what "clean and safe" means can vary by agency. Most social workers will have a checklist that they fill out during home studies. If you're looking to adopt an infant or child under five, that list will be different from the requirements for older children and teens. Ask your agency or professional for a copy of the checklist in advance. Don't get too upset about this checklist; no one expects you to have a fully furnished nursery or preschooler room ready to go or a completely childproofed home. Very few people are rejected based on the home study.

Alert!

Keep things in perspective when it comes to your home study. Don't get bogged down with worry about too many details. Vacuuming and dusting before the social worker arrives is probably appropriate, but having the house repainted or remodeled is probably not.

Some adoption agencies have health codes that require your house to have a minimum square footage for each member of the family, which might necessitate enlarging your living room or adding on a bedroom. However, many agencies are only concerned that the house is large enough to allow separate bedrooms for boys and girls. In addition, each child should have her own bed, but you don't have to have walk-in closets and attached baths. The requirements are very basic and simple, and your agency will work with you to solve any problems.

The Court Process

Once you've completed all the paperwork and have a child selected for you, you will need to work through the courts to get your adoption finalized. The birth parents or state will need to give legal consent for the adoption. In some states, a birth mother has the option of revoking her consent within a certain time period, so you may have to wait through that as well. If you are adopting a child that was an at-risk placement, you will have to wait for parental rights to be terminated. If you are adopting internationally, you will have to work through the foreign court and meet immigration requirements before bringing your child home and beginning an adoption pro-ceeding in your home state. Remember that the court process is not a trial in any way. The court wants to finalize your adoption, and must simply be sure that all legalities are met.

Preparing Yourself Financially

You might think that the hardest financial part of your adoption is behind you with the payment of fees to your agency and lawyer, sup-port of a birth mother, or purchasing tickets to travel to another coun-try. Think about how you will respond and what resources you might tap into if, for example, you lose your job or your child develops a serious illness.

Accessing Help from Specialized Sources

You might want to work with a financial advisor or planner to help you decide if you should buy a home or add on to the one you have, whether your savings are sufficient to cover emergencies, how to save for college, and whether you have enough life and disability insurance to cover the extra costs of a larger family. A financial advisor can be your banker, broker, or insurance agent. Consider asking someone in your adoption support group for a recommendation if you do not currently have a financial advisor.

 Fact

It can be very helpful to plan out what your family expenses will be once your child arrives. Adding a child to your family does not have to mean adding a lot of expenses; if you have older children, you can rely on toys, clothes, and equipment you already have. Begin to think about the long-term expenses the adoption will mean for your family

Don't forget to read your employee handbook and meet with your employer's human resource director. This person can be very helpful in giving you suggestions for dealing with unexpected career and income issues that might occur after the adoption. For example, your company may have a disability policy in place that covers you. You may also get paid or unpaid time off for the adoption (be sure to ask about the federal Family and Medical Leave Act), just as you would for a birth. Your employer may also offer Flexible Spending Accounts for medical and day care expenses.

Financial Help

If you adopt an older child or a special needs child through a state agency, ongoing financial subsidies are often available from your state. Although they won't cover everything your child needs, they could be very helpful. If you adopt through the foster care system, you will probably have access to medical care through the state for the child, even if you have medical insurance through your work or a private policy.

 Essential

In public agency adoptions, many states cover therapy and psychological counseling for the family as well as for the child. However, it is important to understand that state governments do not necessarily have an obligation to provide services to adoptive families for private and or international adoptions.

Other resources include a one-time federal income-tax credit of more than $10,000, Social Security benefits, and more. You can find more information and suggestions in Chapter 12.

Finding the Right Child for You

Adoption is filled with choices. One of them is deciding which child is right for you. Your search will be successful if you think beyond the obvious and are clear on your emotional strengths and weaknesses.

Deciding on an Age Range
Infants less than a year old usually find adjusting to a new family easier than older children, unless they were prenatally exposed to alcohol or drugs. Toddlers (children between the ages of one and three) can find adjustment much more difficult. Because of their limited vocabularies, you cannot use words to help them understand their situation and all the confusing things happening to them. Children over three can have a variety of reactions to adoption, most

often based upon significant experiences with previous placements, as well as other factors.

Consider how everybody's ages in the family will mesh. Maybe your ten-year-old son has a large room where a brother close to his age would fit. But a teenager wouldn't work, because your son is very proud of being the oldest.

If you are under forty and have no other children, you may want a young child. If you already have children or if you are over forty-five, you may want to adopt older children who will fit into the structure of your family or who won't require the exhaustive physical effort demanded by infants.

If you are interested in a newborn, you may choose to look for a birth mother who is going to place her baby for adoption; however, the number of healthy newborns available in the United States continues to decline. You can adopt an infant from another country, but be aware that paperwork and bureaucracies mean he will be closer to a one-year-old when he arrives in your arms; still a baby, but no longer a newborn.

A TEENAGER MIGHT BE PERFECT FOR YOU

You may think that you've postponed considering parenthood too long, that you're too old to qualify for most adoption agencies. While it may be true that beyond your late thirties or early forties you are less likely to be selected by a birth mother (unless you have a kinship or personal relationship with her), you can still consider parenting an older child or teenager.

It is possible that you've heard troubling stories about adolescents, and it's true they do have challenges. Although they don't demand the long-term physical care required by small children, they frequently need a concerned adult available to give good advice and provide structure to their complicated lives. With proper support and training, you can add a teen to your family and reap rewards that far outweigh the effort you make.

Thousands of parents take steps every year to adopt children who will shortly become adults, in order to provide continuity and stability within a permanent family. One of the big problems with the foster care system is that once children are eighteen, they are on their own, with no supporting family. Many people are not ready to be completely independent at this young age. Adopting a teen means you will be able to provide love and support for many years still.

 Fact

You can help solve the problem of too many young people adrift without the moorings of a family. Go to *www.dave thomasfoundationforadoption.org* to get more information from the organization founded by the man who earned a fortune franchising Wendy's fast food restaurants. Dave Thomas, himself an adoptee, said his mission in life was to "assure a safe and loving adoptive home for every child in need."

Gender

Another important decision is what gender you want the child you adopt to be. If you're single, you might want to adopt a child of your own gender. Or, you may want to give your daughter a sister, because siblings of the same gender often establish close relationships. On the other hand, siblings of different genders can be easier to raise because they don't compete as much.

Special Needs

You may be interested in adopting a child with special needs. There are many children in foster care with mental and physical special needs. Some parents find they are very comfortable with the idea of adopting a child who may need extra care. The level of care and attention the newest member of the family will require should be balanced against what the others already in the house need. A child with learning disabilities or physical disabilities might work fine in your home if your other children are self-sufficient. But if you already have a special needs child, another may add unacceptable stress. See Chapter 12 for more information.

Race and Ethnicity

If you love the idea of adding a child from a different background to your family, adopting a child internationally or adopting a foster care child of a different background might appeal to you. Some parents find it exciting to incorporate a different culture or heritage into their family. Other parents feel more comfortable adopting a child who has a similar background. Whatever you choose, there are children available to you. See Chapter 5 for more information about transracial adoptions.

Sibling Groups

There are many sibling groups in foster care and orphanages waiting for homes. State agencies make an effort to place siblings together so they can continue their relationship. Adopting a sibling group is a big commitment; not only do you need more space and resources, you must be prepared to welcome children into your home who have a shared history. As in any family with more than one child, you may find you are more attuned to or comfortable with one of the children. If this situation does occur, you would need to work on making sure all of the siblings felt they had an accepted place in the family.

Stay Flexible and Let Your Heart Lead

While you should carefully consider what type of child would fit best into your family, be willing to keep an open mind—being flexible will help you avoid a lot of frustration. One family described their search for a sister for their daughter Katie, who they had adopted as a newborn and was now three years old. They had already had one adoption fall through and were considering their options, when friends of theirs who were foster parents welcomed a one-year-old girl into their foster family. She was soon freed for adoption, but their friends were unable to adopt her. Katie's parents decided to adopt her, and today, Katie and her little sister Hannah adore each other and are part of a happy family—one the parents never could have predicted.

Every day, more people are experiencing the special joy of adoption. Hopefully, one day soon, enough individuals, couples, and families will be found to give every child the opportunity to be part of a loving family.

CHAPTER 4

Open Versus Closed Adoptions

Closed adoptions, in which birth parents' identities or information are not disclosed, were the norm a generation ago; the privacy of all involved was carefully guarded. Today, however, more than half of all U.S. adoptions are considered open to some degree. Open adoption can mean many things, but at the minimum means that the adoptive parents receive information about the birth parents' histories and identities. The number of open adoptions is growing, but the questions and problems are also growing. Every state handles the matter differently, so be sure you get legal counsel before you decide one way or the other.

Ramifications for Children and Families

People who are involved with adoption make up the triad of adoption: the adoptee, the birth parents, and the adoptive parents. While everybody in the triad is important, the child, the one who has no choice, is the one whose needs should be put ahead of everyone else's. You may want to parent more than anything in the world and the birth parents may think they are unable to do the job, but what is best for a particular child should be of overriding concern.

Reasons for Adoption May Determine Closed or Open

A child becoming available for adoption happens for many reasons, ranging from a voluntary relinquishment to the state stepping in and ending parental rights. In some cases, you won't have a choice about whether the adoption is open or closed. Children who have been abandoned or whose parents have lost their rights because of neglect, abuse, or criminal activity will be in closed adoptions for safety reasons. Many private agency and independent adoptions are open. International adoptions can be closed or open; however, the amount of information available in open cases varies greatly. Kinship adoptions are usually open, since the child is part of the same family unit.

The scenario with the most positive outcomes, according to many adoptees and birth and adoptive parents, is when everybody agrees on what's best for the child. Get some professional advice, talk to your family, and talk to others who have adopted or been adopted. When you make up your mind, be very careful that you don't agree to an open adoption just because you think that's the way you'll get a particular baby. Open adoptions only work if everybody involved is committed to the relationship and understands the benefits and limitations.

What Open Adoption Means

Open adoptions can mean many things. In some situations, the birth and adoptive parents might exchange basic information and then have no ongoing contact. The other end of the spectrum includes the birth parents becoming a regular part of the child's life, with a set role in the child's life. Many families find a middle road, such as sending the birth mother photos and an update once a year.

In open adoptions, the birth mother (possibly with the consent and/or assistance of the biological father) selects the adoptive couple, through an agency or a lawyer specializing in adoptions. Hopeful couples or singles seeking to adopt provide resumes and pictures from which the birth mom selects two or three, interviews them, and makes her choice. Through this process she gets to know the adoptive parents. Some adoptive parents go along on doctor appointments or are present in the delivery room. Each birth mother and adoptive parent team must work out what they are comfortable with and what will work for them.

Alert!

Your child's history is personal and deserves respect. If you're in an open adoption, don't make the mistake of thinking open means you have to give the checkout clerk details about your child's life. There's a distinction between healthy openness and legitimate privacy. This is even more true if your adoption is closed because of abuse or neglect.

Until just a year or two ago, open adoptions were not protected by law; they were informal contracts that could only be enforced by agreement of both parties. Today, some states have passed laws enforcing open-adoption contracts, and you still have the choice of whether or not to enter into one.

Open Adoption Advantages

The greatest advantage in an open adoption is knowing the physical and genetic history of your child. This will be important for medical reasons, but also to give your child a sense of history. You may also find that you can connect with members of the birth family and empathize with them.

Essential

The extended birth family can give unique attention to your adopted child, attention that can help make up for a sense of loss he might feel. Michelle, the adopted mom of David, received an heirloom baby quilt from his biological great-grandmother that her grandmother had knitted, "So he has a blanket from his great, great, great-grandmother, something not many kids can claim."

Joy and Kurt were delighted about the open adoption of their son. In the years since the birth, they have continued to have a relationship with their son's birth father and the birth father's mother and sister, who come for birthday parties, send Christmas gifts, and call or e-mail. They are happy that their son has a connection to his birth family, and they don't feel overwhelmed by the amount of contact.

Open Adoption Disadvantages

If your arrangement with the birth parents or extended family includes in-person visits, you may fear that your child will love her birth parents more, especially if she only sees those parents or relatives occasionally or on vacations or holidays. Remember, though, that the real challenges and rewards of parenting are the day-to-day things; visiting and sending presents is not parenting.

One problem with open adoptions is that you must consent to a plan that may not end up working or being comfortable. If you and the birth mom have a falling out, a yearly visit from her could feel very intrusive and uncomfortable. This is why it is important to be cautious and only agree to what you know you can honor. Often, families find open adoption easier when the child is still very young and does not have a complete understanding of adoption. As a child gets older, questions about adoption and his biological parents' adoption decision can create conflicted feelings, making continued contact with his biological parent or parents difficult.

Alert!

Open adoption is not for the weak or timid. It is not easy to have a relationship with a broken-hearted birth mom and other relatives. You will find it hard to deal with their pain when you're feeling joy and happiness, but remember that you cannot take responsibility for the biological family's emotions.

All open adoptions are a consensual agreement between both parties; they're a choice that you must weigh carefully. The arrangement is doomed to fail if either party backs out or doesn't live up to the agreed-upon terms.

If the birth parents make commitments to you for visitation and don't keep them, your child will experience a double whammy. She will be upset both for the missed visit or phone call and with you for allowing the problem to happen in the first place.

Figuring out how often and when to allow visits by biological family members can be complicated. Most adoptive families have very limited contact with the birth parents—many do not allow an in-person relationship to develop between child and birth parent during childhood. If you and the birth parent have agreed to frequent visits, remember that the ties to your family are the primary relationship—visits with biological family should never interfere with the attachments you are building. It's very important that your child not be confused about who her parents are or what family she belongs in. As the parent, you must monitor contact and always keep your child's well-being uppermost in your mind.

What Closed Adoption Means

Closed adoption generally means that the adoptive parents do not know the identity of the birth parents. This does not mean that the identity will forever remain unknown; many adult adoptees are able to find their birth parents. Sometimes, this requires intensive searching; in other cases, the adoption agency may have a mutual-consent program in place—if both the birth parent and the child wish to find each other, their information will be shared.

Some adult adoptees of closed adoptions say they have no interest in finding their birth families because they feel that it doesn't matter who their birth parents are since they have real parents in their adoptive parents. Other adult adoptees report that they worried about where they came from or wondered what their birth families looked like. The unknown history can be very haunting. Others wanted only to satisfy curiosity, to find out why they were placed for adoption, or to let the birth parents know they were grateful to have been adopted by "fantastic parents."

Making an Informed Choice

Deciding whether to do an open or closed adoption is an extremely important choice. Talk to others who have been or are in open or closed adoptions, take as much training as possible and read books, and think carefully about what will work best for you and your family. By thinking it out and educating yourself on your options, you can make a more informed decision.

One mother said that when she and her husband adopted the first time, open adoption was really pushed on them. With all of the attachment issues they subsequently dealt with, they were very glad their adoption turned out to be closed. They sent the birth mom letters through the agency for the first few years, but she never acknowledged receipt or contacted them.

In the end, you'll have to make a decision that seems most comfortable to you and works the best for the specific situation you have planned.

Trust Your Instincts as You Choose

Remember the most crucial aspect of raising any child, adopted or biological: You are the parent and you have the ethical and legal right to make decisions. Family members, educators, and therapists may give you counsel, but you should only follow advice that coincides with your basic moral framework. Trust your instincts, and don't let others distract you or make you question your parenting skills.

Gather Information, No Matter What

Whether you opt for a closed or open adoption, it is important that you gather as much information as you can about your child and his family's history. For medical reasons, you will want to be able to have as complete a history as possible about illnesses and conditions in the family, as well as about your child's health before the adoption.

Alert!

In many states, laws that indicate blood relatives have first claim on a child whose parents have had their rights terminated have resulted in children being taken from foster homes where they've formed attachments to the foster parents and placed with strangers who happened to be biological kin. Such placements have a high potential for serious emotional harm to the children.

Gather information about the biological family that your child has a right to know and may request when he's an adult. Collect and preserve as much information as you can and share it with him at appropriate times. Almost all adopted children eventually become curious about where they came from. Any information you can glean, such as physical characteristics, family nationality, or interests will be precious information to your child. If you recognize your child's curiosity and support her feelings about this, you will strengthen your attachment over the years.

Working closely with a professional therapist who specializes in adoption can be helpful in establishing guidelines regarding information sharing. An adoptive mom of three described how sad she felt that she didn't know her children's heritage like she knew her own. Although her children connected with their adoptive family, including extended relatives, they had questions about their birth families that she just couldn't answer.

Emotional Considerations for Making a Decision

Making the decision about an open or closed adoption requires both logic and emotions, so you must be willing to devote time to the decision. If you get into a situation where the birth mom wants an open relationship and you're uncomfortable with the idea, don't agree just because you desperately want a baby.

Seek out adoptive-parent groups where you can meet parents who will understand and support your dilemma and who can offer their own perspectives on this issue. The National Adoption Clearinghouse publishes a National Adoption Directory with state-by-state listings of adoption agencies, parent groups, and other organizations.

Consider How Your Child Will Be Affected

Authorities and experienced adoptive parents agree that very young children can become confused if a definite line isn't drawn between the parent and birth parent. The age of the child is crucial; when your child is young, she should be able to settle into your family and gain a sense of belonging without confusion over who her parents are. There's an old saying that "too many cooks spoil the broth," meaning that when too many people have authority to make decisions, conflicts can ensue. In the same way, too many parents can damage your child's emotional development.

You should also consider how your child will feel without any contact or information about her birth family. This is the flip side of the coin, and another situation you must consider in your decision.

Consider How You Will Create Attachment

As mentioned earlier, your family must be your child's primary place to grow up. Others can support and help you, and lots of people can love your child as extended family, but only you and your spouse or partner should make the important decisions while your child is young.

You must think about how an open or closed adoption will impact the family you are creating. Consider these kinds of questions:

- How will you cope with a birth mother in an open adoption who regrets her decision?
- How will you handle questions from a child who does not understand why her birth parents are unknown?
- What will you do if a birth father begins to demand more and more visits with your child?
- How will you explain a biological grandmother who is very involved, but then suddenly backs out of the situation?
- What might you do if you realize several months into an open adoption that it makes you very uncomfortable?
- If a birth parent acted inappropriately and you needed to cut off contact, how would you explain that to your child who has developed a rewarding relationship with her?

These are the kinds of possible scenarios you should ponder when weighing open versus closed adoption.

Explaining Your Decision to Family and Friends

Adopting a child impacts not just you, but your whole extended family, your spouse, and other children if you have them. While choosing to adopt a child is essentially a personal, private decision, your new child will come into a new family that will affect him deeply, and vice versa. When you adopt a child or children, your entire extended family's culture will change.

 Essential

Celebrate your changing culture right from the start. Send out announcements and have a party. Then, when the adoption becomes final, invite your family to court to witness the process and go out to lunch or dinner afterward.

Explaining an Open Adoption

You might be asked by family or friends to explain your decision to have an open adoption. Be aware that there is a chance they may not react as you wish. They may think you're being foolish and exposing yourself and your child to potential dangers.

Alert!

Research and some anecdotal evidence indicate that adoptive parents in semi-open adoptions are more fearful about birth families than those in either completely open or closed adoptions. The reason could be that semi-open is a sort of a compromise that may not satisfy either party.

Rehearse a simple explanation about why you chose an open adoption that you can use when somebody who has a right to know asks questions. However, don't get into a debate or argument about your particular decision. Sometimes, it's best to say, "I appreciate your concern, but we thought long and hard and know this is right for us."

Explaining Why You Chose a Closed Adoption

Closed adoptions are still the norm for nearly half of all domestic and most international adoptions for many reasons, especially for children adopted through the foster care system. Your family and friends may ask for details about your child's past, but remember that your child deserves privacy, and sharing information about a birth parent's conduct that resulted in the termination of rights is only appropriate for those with a need to know. These people may include your pediatrician, your child's teacher, and very close family members. Again, be careful about whom you tell what; once your child is school age, discuss with him what he wants to share with others—it's his choice.

Effects of an Open or Closed Adoption on Existing Children

Whether or not the adoption is open can present unique concerns for siblings. Your biological child may be jealous if your adopted child has an additional set of parents and grandparents, and the situation may drive a wedge in family relationships. The best way to handle this is to explain how the adoption came about and why the new child has birth parents who are involved. It is important to stress that the new child is an equal member of the family, even though he may have birth parents that are somehow involved. Explain that it does not make him any less of a family member to have these ties to other people.

A closed adoption might seem mysterious to existing children, who may ply you with questions about the new child's history. All you can do is give age-appropriate answers rooted in honesty. Siblings can also take advantage of a closed adoption to taunt the other child or make up wild stories that the adoptive child will believe. It is up to you to make sure everyone in the family understands what the truth is, but you have to remember that siblings frequently find something to tease each other about, and an adoption is just one more factor.

Explaining Your Choice to Your Child

As you raise your child, you will likely spend a lot of time talking about the adoption, answering your child's questions, and discussing the situation. Whether the adoption was open or closed is just a small part of that discussion. When your child is old enough, you can explain the difference between the two choices, and why the choice was made in his situation. From the very beginning, though, you can talk about your child's birth mother, and possibly father, in a way that relates to the open or closed nature of the adoption.

If your adoption is closed, you can tell your child about a birth mother who loved him but wasn't able to raise him. In an open adoption, what you say will depend on the relationship with the birth mother.

Studies and Legal Changes on Open Adoptions

Adoption laws are continually being written and rewritten. The movement toward open adoption continues to build and courts and agencies are responding to that trend.

Studies Reveal Important Findings

The effects of open adoption on children are being studied, and some interesting data are coming out. Studies at the University of Minnesota, the University of California, Stanford, and others demonstrate that most children in both open and closed adoptions are well adjusted and do well in school, with no distinction between the two groups.

Open adoptions are still too new to determine long-term impact on adoptees that grow up and start families of their own.

Adoption Laws

Many states are creating open-record laws that make it possible for an adult adoptee to access her birth information. This is not quite the same thing as an open adoption, where the birth parent is known to the child throughout her life.

The United Nations and UNICEF came up with a treaty in 1991 that was ratified by eighty-one countries, most recently by the United States in 2007. The Treaty of the International Rights of the Child states that all children have a right to know where they come from, to meet their family, and to know their heritage, which supports the idea of open adoptions.

This treaty and the Convention on Protection of Children and Co-Operation in Respect of Inter-Country Adoption (usually referred to as the Hague Adoption Convention) are part of the impetus for open adoptions and the moving away from closed adoptions. However, open adoptions still aren't the norm, and the debate will continue. Whether you have an open or closed adoption remains, for now, a matter of personal choice.

CHAPTER 5

Adoption Outside Your Ethnic Group

If you are considering adopting a child who doesn't come from your same ethnic background, you need to explore the psychological and emotional ramifications of such an adoption. You should understand the difference between race and culture and develop a plan for addressing issues arising from those differences. While all adoptive parents need education and support, you may also face prejudices and legal biases that can be extremely frustrating unless you're well prepared.

The Implications of Race Versus Culture

The term "ethnicity" involves both race and culture. "Race" means a person's genetic make up and is categorized by the United States Bureau of the Census as White, Black or African American, American Indian or Alaska Native, Asian, or Some Other Race. It involves skin and eye color, hair texture, and other distinctive racial features. Ethnicity involves cultural background, such as Hispanic, Jewish, or Arab. There are hundreds of possible ethnic identifications. "Culture" means lifestyle, traditions, and behaviors that may have nothing to do with genetics, but are often distinct between groups of people.

As an adoptive parent, you should focus on the fact that culture is more important than race in shaping character: Culture is a chosen behavior; race is a physical characteristic beyond anyone's control. Your choices about blending your child's heritage into your family's culture will shape your future together in unique ways. The main point you need to keep in mind is that while biology is important, environment and culture will determine who your child becomes.

The Breakdown of Racial Barriers

World War II, the Korean Conflict, Vietnam, and the civil rights movement have had a big impact on attitudes toward race in this country. Soldiers brought home war brides from Korea and Japan, and society began to understand how unimportant racial features were in determining intrinsic worth. The civil rights movement drove home the point that we are all the same. The fact that the world is becoming a smaller place due to modern travel and communication has opened up world trade and interaction and allowed people to learn about other cultures and heritages more easily.

Some prominent people (as well as everyday people) from African American, Korean, Native American, or Hispanic heritages are challenging those who insist on classifying them as one particular race or another. As society progresses and science learns more about the realities of genetic and environmental influences, these artificial barriers between peoples will become less and less important. We are, after all, each physically different from each other. The traits that some people seem to pinpoint as racial characteristics (such as skin color, eye shape, and so on) do not have to stop family members who are racially different from feeling close and accepted by each other.

However, children who recognize their racial differences within a family or community can have negative, conflicted feelings at some time during their developmental years. Parents must be willing to acknowledge and help resolve these difficult feelings or it can lead to children feeling disconnected from their adoptive family. This is particularly true in the adolescent years, when teens are struggling to establish an identity.

Culture Plays a Major Role in Child Development

The arguments against transracial adoption seem to be mainly about preserving a specific culture rather than about the genetic make up of the child and the prospective parents. Those who argue against it say that by placing a child in a family of a different race, the adoptive child loses his connection with his racial group and heritage, and that group's culture is eroded by this loss.

It is important that you think about the ramifications of this type of adoption. Ask yourself these questions:

- What is my attitude toward the culture of my child's biological family?
- How will my extended family respond to a child who is different than they are?
- How will my neighborhood and town react to a child of a particular race?
- What steps will I take to promote attachment and cohesiveness within my family?
- What can I do to help my child feel connected to her cultural and racial background?

As you answer these questions, keep in mind that, according to Gail Steinberg and Beth Hall, experts in the field of transracial adoptions, children adopted by parents from a different race live with two racial realities—one from their family of origin and one from the family they are adopted into. These children can't choose between their families and their race without experiencing serious psychological harm. As an adoptive parent, it's your job to make sure your child never has to choose, and that she can accept and live with both realities.

Good News about Transracial Adoption

A study by Rita Simon and Howard Alstein came up with some conclusions that should be very reassuring for you. The adoptive parents who were still in the study after their children were grown were asked, "Thinking back, and with the knowledge of hindsight and the experiences you have accumulated, would you have done what you did—

adopt a child of a different race?" Ninety-two percent said "Yes," 4 percent said "Not sure," and 4 percent said, "No." A high percentage of the adoptive parents would have adopted outside their ethnic group again, even knowing the challenges and problems they would face.

 Essential

Become aware of specifics about your child's heritage such as how African American parents groom their children's hair. The grooming a parent does for any child demonstrates to the world how loved and special she is, but it's especially significant for a White parent with an African American child.

Adopted adults in the study "Adoption across Borders" were asked if they thought being from a different racial background from their siblings and parents affected their relationships, and almost 90 percent said it didn't matter one way or the other. The researchers also found that the transracially adopted adults were just as likely to turn to their parents or siblings for help and support as the White adoptees or biological children in their families.

A twenty-year study of transracial adoptions (386 black children and the 204 white families who adopted them) by sociologist Rita Simon of American University in Washington, D. C., and Howard Altstein of the University of Maryland indicated that children generally do well with adoptive parents of another race and that "transracial adoption causes no special problems. In fact, it may produce adults who possess superior interpersonal skills and talents."

Think about Your Own Motives

Adopting a child who is ethnically different from you requires you to become educated about what that other ethnicity entails. Having a heart full of love and wanting to build your family through adoption are prerequisites, but adoption is a unique adventure and can get complicated, even without the added challenge of parenting a child from a different ethnic background.

You might feel motivated to rescue an institutionalized child or a teenager who's aging out of the foster care system or an older child who is in another country's orphanage. Such positive and powerful motives should be tempered with education and research, as well as a clear-eyed assessment of your own strengths and weaknesses for taking on such a complicated challenge. It is one thing to want to do good in the world and another to live in a family that faces the challenges of a transracial adoption. You need to think not only about what your beliefs are, but about what kind of family you are most comfortable building and supporting. If you believe a transracial adoption would be too challenging for you, that is the right decision for you and you can certainly adopt a child of your own race instead.

Attitudes and Pressure from Relatives

Your extended family's preconceived ideas will either help or hinder your choice to adopt a child of a different race. Stephanie, an adoptive mom in Missouri, said that she and her husband, Rudy, faced stiff resistance from his family when they adopted their son, who is half Black and half Native American. Rudy's grandfather told them that they should "stick to their own kind" and had no business "doing this to the family." But when Nicky toddled up to him and grinned, "Hi, Gupa," he melted and they've been best buddies ever since.

Your challenge with family members who resist a transracial adoption is to lovingly educate them and try not to take comments to heart. However, if family members are openly hostile or even just cool toward your child, tell them that their behavior is unacceptable and that there will be no contact until the behavior changes. If, in addition to the transracial child, you have biological children or adopted children who are of your own race, this stance is critical. Your child is your first priority, and a relative's feelings are secondary.

 Essential

Studies demonstrate that African Americans who are adopted by White families date people from various ethnic groups and have more friends from other groups than either their White or Black friends. Check out *www.adoptivefamilies.com/transracial* for excellent tips and readings from parents who adopted across racial lines.

Strategies for Parenting a Racially Different Child

Your challenge will be to demonstrate to your child that you cherish her differences because they are part of what makes her a special individual. Short or tall, fair or dark skinned, curly or straight haired, a child's physical appearance should be taken for granted; never say anything that disparages characteristics that cannot be changed.

Stress how your child is similar to you and the rest of the family. Come up with two or three similarities for every difference that you comment on, so your child can feel firmly connected to her place in your family. For example, you might say, "Your hair and eyes are darker than mine, but we both love strawberry shortcake and you and Dad like to watch the Discovery Channel together." These kinds of statements emphasize your similarities and your bond as a family unit.

Your child makes your family different; be ready to deal with the reactions of people who are uncomfortable with or even afraid of differences. If you and your family obviously enjoy not only your own blended culture, but others as well, you will provide a positive example to your extended family and community.

Alert!

Although most people in the adoption world believe it is more crucial to find homes for children that need them than to limit adoptions within races, there are some impediments. The Indian Child Welfare Act (ICWA) mandates that every attempt be made to place a Native American child into a Native American home. Groups such as the National Association of Black Social Workers (NABSW) have taken a public stand that adoption be along racial lines, "unless no other situation is possible."

Helping Your Child Connect with Her Heritage

By demonstrating that you are interested in the cultural heritage of your child, you are accepting everything about her. You are also validating her lineage and her physical realities. Doing so may not be easy, but it will be worthwhile.

Try to find an adult who comes from the same culture as your child. For example, if your daughter is Black, enlist the help of Black friends as mentors. Your child needs to see other faces and body types similar to hers, especially as she becomes an adolescent. There are many ways to help your child connect to her cultural or ethnic heritage. You could:

- Celebrate Chinese New Year (or other cultural holidays) each year with traditional foods.
- Buy books about your child's country of origin and read them to her.
- Attend an ethnic festival together, such as Cinco de Mayo or Kwanzaa.
- Plan a family vacation to your child's country of origin.

Some families make an effort to incorporate celebrations and traditions from many countries, ethnicities, and races into their family, so that they can all feel truly connected to people all over the world.

Talk about Differences

Some adoptive parents worry that separating their children's specific heritage interferes with family solidarity and bonding, but talking about differences can be helpful. Adoptive father Sam said that his son, Brett, was two when adopted. With his dark skin and straight black hair, he was obviously not born to fair-haired Sam and his wife. Sometimes, Brett would put his hand on top of Sam's and say, "You and I are different colors." Sam would answer, "Yes, we are. Your Indian birth mom gave you that great tan." Then they'd go on with what they'd been doing. Sam says that he never notices Brett's physical differences and loves all his children equally.

 Essential

Your heritage will be important and become part of your child's own heritage. Your child will grow up eating your family's foods and celebrating your holidays. These things will belong to her just as they belong to you. With a little encouragement and enthusiasm, you can let your child know that she is a very real part of your cultural line, while still helping her feel a part of her birth family's heritage.

Don't Focus Exclusively on Differences

Most experts, as well as many adoptive parents of grown children, caution against overemphasizing your child's racial heritage over your family's culture. You should trust your instincts and knowledge of your own child as you raise her to be the best person she can be. Don't go overboard—take your clues from your child, especially as she approaches adolescence. In the words of one twelve-year-old Hispanic girl, "Why does every meal have to be about something? Let's just be normal!"

 **Fact**

Every race and culture has unique and special things to offer. Talk about George Washington Carver, Chief Joseph, Martin Luther King Jr., Cesar Chavez, and others so they become personal heroes and not just figures in a history book. Try to make sure your children have friends that are of the same race as well as other races.

Adolescents can be very sensitive about being made to feel different. Some children will express curiosity about their birth families at this time and others will prefer to settle into their school and social lives. They may even become hostile if you bring up their culture outside your family, and you may have to back off. There are many resources available to you for learning and teaching about a specific heritage. An annotated list is included in Appendix A.

Experienced adoption professionals and adult adoptees advise you to really get to know your child, to observe her and figure out how she's different from and similar to you in personality, and not make assumptions based on her heritage. They suggest you consider such things as her taste in food and music, whether she has a relaxed or intense personality, her body type, etc. As you notice differences, you should acknowledge them in a loving, validating way, just as you would notice and cherish differences between you and your biological children. Your children, adopted or biological, are totally different people from each other and from you. Be careful not to overemphasize distinctions, or your child may feel odd and disconnected.

Claiming Rituals

When children are born, relatives look at the peacefully sleeping or squalling infant and say such things as, "He's got Aunt Bessie's temper," "There's Daddy's nose," or "Look at those shoulders—he'll play football, like Uncle Ben." Therapists call this activity claiming, a way for the family to enfold the newcomer and take ownership of him. If your child is adopted, you may feel as if he is being left out of this claiming process. However, as relatives become more accepting of an adopted family member, they frequently find ways to connect the child's behaviors or characteristics to the family.

 Essential

> Try to find people who were adopted and raised by parents from different ethnic backgrounds. Meeting adults and being with other children who have been or are going through the same experience can be validating and pleasant for your child. You can find resources online through the National Adoption Information Clearinghouse and by accessing a search engine using "Adoption China," "Adoption Guatemala," etc.

You can do the same with your ethnically different child. Pointing out similarities in behavior or appearance helps your child and you connect and reinforces the bond to relatives and friends. Claiming is important. Jake was White and had two biological sons when he adopted Alex, an African American baby boy. He was happy to hear his biological sons saying things like, "Alex likes to suck his thumb just like I did" and "Look Daddy, Alex loves the kitty like we do!"

Develop Your Child's Social Skills

You and your child should be prepared to face prejudice and ignorance about your adoption. No matter how much you love your child and how color blind you may be, you must equip her with the social skills she'll need to function in a society that still has racist components. In doing so, you can help her develop confidence and pride in her ethnic heritage. That pride can be part of her identity as a unique member of the family.

Create Connections

Most parents report that the main challenge they face is not knowing quite what to do. A study at the University of Texas involved two groups of thirty African American middle-class adolescents, one group adopted by Black families, the other by White families. The researchers concluded that the most successful transracial outcomes were when White adoptive parents had ties to the Black community, lived in integrated neighborhoods, and sent their children to integrated schools. This study shows that if you can create a family that has connections to other racial groups, your child will benefit from it.

Being active with a support group can help you, especially if you can meet together and introduce your children to one another. So-called "culture camps" have popped up around the country where school-aged and adolescent children adopted from India, the Ukraine, Korea, and other countries can meet other children adopted from their particular region. These camps advertise online and in publications like *Adoptive Families Magazine*.

Dealing with Racism

You may find out, as many adoptive parents have reported, that the racism and biases you encounter come from all races. It can be quite shocking to realize that people of all colors and backgrounds can hold these divisive beliefs.

You will be challenged to equip your racially different child to deal with racism without the bitterness that can only escalate problems. Society is gradually becoming more accepting of mixed heritages and biracial families, but your child may still be the focus of some sort of racist comment or attitude at some point, especially if you live in a community that isn't very diverse. Stand behind your child; don't fight her battles, but give her the tools to handle hurt or anger. Pretending this kind of situation will never happen is neither realistic nor helpful.

Question?

How can I handle an upsetting confrontation when my child is too young to understand the words but senses the hostility?

First, walk away from it without causing a scene if you can. Children under age five or six can be reassured afterward with a hug and a dismissive, "That person was certainly upset, huh?" from you. They will follow your lead: If you don't act agitated or like something is wrong, they won't pay much attention.

Role-playing can be very effective, especially if you have input from friends of color. Act out a situation with your child in which someone says a racially inappropriate comment. Suggest ways to handle it and allow your child to practice. It can be helpful to discuss with an older child what kinds of racial slurs she might hear—you wouldn't want your child to be caught unaware by a name she has never heard before.

Modeling is another way to help your child. Allow her to see how you respond to comments or behaviors that negatively comment on race or biracial families. Hearing and observing how you respond will give your child a good example of what to do. In addition, interact with other parents who've adopted transracially; your child needs relationships with other children who are in the same situation as she is.

The Ultimate Responsibility Rests with You

You can't control how other people react to your adoption and your child, but you can control how you react. Raising your child with love and pride is one small but important step in changing people's attitudes. Surviving the process emotionally and legally requires you to have a strong sense of self-worth and a clear understanding of your personal values, with the ability to translate your values into behavior that allows your children to thrive.

CHAPTER 6

International Adoptions

International adoptions have become more popular recently, partially because of the perception (not entirely wrong) that few babies are available domestically, and that there are many awaiting adoption in other countries. Some adoptive parents fear that U.S. birth families could find the child more readily and disrupt the adoption, even years later. Another reason for the escalating number of international adoptions is the spread of multiculturalism: More and more people are embracing the value of all peoples.

Deciding to Adopt Internationally

There are many reasons to choose an international adoption—you feel a connection to a certain country, you would like to adopt a young child but don't want to go through being matched with a U.S. birth mother, you are entranced with the idea of expanding your family to include a child from another country, or you feel a responsibility to step up and make a difference in the life of a child.

To be able to have a successful international adoption, you should be able to answer the following questions:

- How will I help my child bridge two cultures and languages?
- How will my other children, extended family, and community respond?

- What steps will I take to promote attachment and enhance our family's unique culture?
- How will I cope with a child who may have been neglected or abused?

All four of these questions can apply to domestic adoptions, but they have a special urgency when you consider that your child will be coming into a completely alien world.

You also must consider your own personality and abilities. Some children who are adopted internationally may be hyperactive, oppositionally defiant, or just simply very challenged if their early days were difficult. Think honestly about whether you are equipped to deal with a child who may have delays or behavioral problems.

Some children from international orphanages may have developmental delays or experience severe attachment difficulties depending upon their ages and experiences. Lack of good prenatal care or use of alcohol and or drugs by the mother while pregnant can lead to difficulties for the child such as Fetal Alcohol Syndrome or learning disabilities. It is not uncommon for agencies to fail to be completely honest with adoptive parents about a child's history or tendencies, so it is important to get as much information as possible, including expert evaluations of any child you are considering. As a prospective adoptive parent, you do not have to let these possibilities dissuade you from adopting a child; rather, you can educate yourself and enter into such an adoption with as much forethought and knowledge as possible to approach your child's special needs proactively.

Choosing a Country

The countries most open to U.S. citizens adopting changes periodically, as does the red tape involved. Experienced parents who have adopted from another country and experts such as the Holt Adoption Agency (one of the United States' most senior and respected agencies) all caution prospective parents to work with a reputable agency or facilitator. It's virtually impossible to go it alone due to language barriers, bureaucratic procedures, and cultural differences. Check the U.S. Department of State Web site at *http://travel.state.gov/family/ adoption/adoption_485.html* for details for current countries open to U.S. adoption.

As you ponder which country you wish to approach, consider whether you have personal ties or specific interest in any area of the world. You will want to consider the health care that is available in the countries you are considering and whether the children available are from foster care or orphanages. Research the type of care that is provided at orphanages by doing Internet searches and talking with parents who have adopted from that country.

The process in some countries is easier than in others; the agency you select should help you with the pros and cons of countries with available children. Requirements on your religion, marital status, age, number of children already in your home, and even your weight will vary from country to country. Some of the most adoption-friendly countries as of this book's writing were: Ethiopia, India, China, Guatemala, Kazakhstan, Ukraine, and South Korea. Be sure to check the political or social situation in the country you are considering.

 Fact

International adoptions have declined in China, Russia, and South Korea over the past two years, although thousands of children still come to the United States from these countries. On the other hand, adoptions are up by almost 40 percent in Ethiopia, to 1,255 in 2007 from 732 in 2006.

Because of its population limits, China has been a steady source of infants and young children for U.S. parents for many years. However, China has recently stopped permitting single-parent adoption. Russia has designated every child born there as having Russian citizenship, and is making a concerted effort to stop the exporting of its children.

Once you choose a country, find out everything you can about it. The Internet has many resources. Learn at least a few key phrases and words of the particular language; although you will have an interpreter, your efforts to communicate in the language of the country will demonstrate your willingness to preserve distinctive parts of your child's culture. This willingness may be an important factor in deciding to grant the adoption.

Selecting and Working with Adoption Professionals

While domestic adoptions can be done privately without an agency, international adoptions should always be through a reputable agency or facilitator. Be sure the agency you choose is licensed in your state, as well as accepted by the country where your child is. It is very important that the agency or facilitator has placed many successful adoptions from the country you are interested in.

 **Alert!**

Keep your agency updated on your moves or address changes. Your agency should not only find you a child, but help you once the child is in your home. Ideally, you will have a continuing relationship that will keep you grounded and provide resources as your family matures.

Ask for references and be sure to call them. Ask the references what their experience was like and about any problems they encountered. Be sure to pick someone with whom you feel comfortable, because your relationship will be intense, personal, and long term.

Ask the following questions before you sign with an agency:

- How many successful adoptions have you sponsored from this country?
- What was the average wait time?
- How long have you been in business?
- Do you have a list of former clients who would be willing to speak to me?
- What kind of preadoption training do you offer? Have your clients been pleased with that training?
- Do you offer postadoption training and follow-up?
- How long do you stay in contact with your families?
- What are your fees? Are any of these fees refundable if the adoption falls through?
- What procedure is followed and services are offered if the adoption does not seem to be working out?

Note that as in all human relationships, there are no real guarantees in adoption. Ask questions and discuss what you find out with your partner or spouse. Don't pick an agency solely on the basis of cost or whether the person you talked to was convincing.

Dealing with Other Languages and Cultures

When you adopt a child from another country, you must be ready to address similar cultural and racial issues as when adopting outside your ethnic group, as well as the addition of language barriers. The country your child comes from may be completely foreign to you, or you may have visited there before. Either way, you must expect many things to be different about the culture. The language barrier will likely be a big one, unless you are bilingual in that language.

Read books about your child's country. Buy tapes to help you learn some of the language, so that you can communicate basic things to your child. Research the customs and traditions of the country and region your child comes from; it's important not only for you to understand them, but to be able to share them with your child when she is older.

The child you bring home will experience new sights, smells, sounds, and sensations. It can be difficult for a child, especially a young child, to adjust to this bombardment of new stimulation. Depending on his developmental age, she may be terrified as well as disoriented. You will struggle to empathize, reassure, and make it possible for your child to attach to you—tasks that won't be easy or simple.

If you adopt from another country, the culture of your child's country and heritage will enrich your family life. In a way, you become a part of that culture yourself when you parent a child from it.

Dealing with Foreign Bureaucracies

Depending on which country you choose, your search for a child can be relatively short and simple or very complicated, lengthy, and even heartbreaking. Because you will be dealing with a foreign country and government that does things in a completely different way, you may find the process to be sometimes confusing and or frustrating. That is partly why a good agency is so important; they will intercede for you and explain to you exactly what to expect so you don't feel so left in the dark.

Your agency will prepare you for exactly what steps you will need to take while completing your adoption. Many foreign governments do not function like the U.S. government; they run on completely different principles, and you should not expect that anything will be fair, swift, or clear. There is nothing you can do to change these processes, so you must simply be prepared to cope with them. In some countries, you can expect to have to bribe some officials, endure long waits, deal with last-minute changes in requirements, or jump through many hoops. A good agency will have someone to help you through every step of the process.

Preparing to Bring Your Child into the United States

Finally being matched with a child and having that child designated as yours are only the first steps in building your family. The more you can do to deal with administrative matters ahead of time, the more quickly you will be able to adjust to one another once you're under the same roof.

Paperwork Is Critical

First, you must make sure that you've taken care of all the paperwork involved, for the United States as well as your adoptive country. Your agency or facilitator will guide you through the process, which includes your dossier, home study, and background check, all of which must be translated. Once you've been cleared by the particular country, you must deal with United States immigration. You must have physically seen the child yourself before you can petition the government to have her classified as an "immediate relative" and acquire her Visa (if you adopt from South Korea, where you need not travel prior to placement, this designation can be made after the child arrives). You will be required to appear with her at the embassy or consular office for an interview. She will also have to be examined by a physician approved by the embassy.

Alert!

Even if the adoption is finalized in your child's original country, you must readopt him in your state court to make it legal in the United States. A most helpful Web site, *www.uscis.gov*, will guide you. Of course, your agency should also be guiding you.

Your child cannot come into the country until the proper paperwork has been processed by the Department of Homeland Security. You will need an attorney to help you with this process—your agency may provide one.

Assessing Your Child

When you first meet your child or first take custody of her, you will want to make sure she is healthy. Make a list of needs that should be assessed: physical, emotional, intellectual, social, and cultural. The American Academy of Pediatrics can help you find a pediatrician who specializes in adoption, and who can then refer you to therapists, social workers, and so on, if needed, in your area. See *www.aap.org/sections/adoption/adopt-states/adoption.map.htm.*

Most adoption specialists recommend that you have your child assessed before you consent to the adoption. That means finding a pediatrician who has experience in doing an assessment from photos or video taken while you are with the prospective adoptive child. While you might be comfortable adopting a child with a disability, special needs, or chronic illness, it is always a good idea to have that information up front so that you know exactly what you are agreeing to.

Handling the Interminable Waiting

In the words of one adoptive father, "Everything is hurry, hurry, wait, wait, wait, hurry, wait, wait, hurry." Waiting may be the hardest part of the whole process, particularly in an international adoption, where you may be matched with a child but then have to wait many months to bring him home. Try not to focus on what you don't have (your child in your home), but instead, make the intervening time productive.

A good resource is Adoption Alliance, Inc.'s international division (*www.adoptall.com*). The group, located in Colorado, is run mostly by volunteers who have adopted internationally. Through them, you can meet others who understand your perspective and situation.

Question?

> **Why is there so much waiting involved in an international adoption?**
> There is no good answer to that question. It takes time for the foreign agency to approve you. It takes time for them to assign you a child. It takes time for your adoption to be processed. And it takes time for immigration papers to be approved. There are delays at every step of the way and no good reason, except that is just how the process works.

Several parents interviewed for this book confided that they believe the waiting, disappointments, and hassles that go with the adoption process are actually an important rite of passage. You slog through the endless forms, bracing yourself against heartbreak, and then somehow emerge on the other side and begin the joy of parenting a unique and wonderful child.

Bond with Your Child as You Wait

Your child has less choice in all this than you do and the delays are much harder on him than they are on you. Even though separated by thousands of miles, you can do many things to establish a bond that will allow your child to attach to you and your family. It can be very difficult to go to an orphanage, meet a child that is designated as yours, and then have to leave him to come home and wait.

You can send your child photos of you and your home or small, soft toys. Today's technology can also be a big help. Take videos of you, your spouse, other children, and the family pets. Tape the outside of your house, the yard, and neighboring homes. You may need to send a VCR for him to watch them on, and you must understand there are no guarantees that this technology will not be stolen by orphanage workers or officials.

Make recordings of your voice, too. Send your child cassette tapes and a tape player. Read stories to him on tape and send along the books they come with so he can follow what you're saying, if he's old enough. Even though he probably doesn't speak English, he'll become familiar with the sound of your voice and English words.

Learn some phrases in his language to introduce the tapes, like, "When you are here with me, I'll read this story to you before you go to sleep." Making the videos and tapes will help you deal with the stress of being separated and the delays that may keep coming up.

Helping Your Child Adjust

Your child may have been nutritionally and cognitively neglected during her early days. No matter what kind situation she is coming out of, she will need consistent, long-term structure to adjust to her new life. She may have learned unacceptable ways of coping with the orphanage or foster home, such as screaming or indiscriminate signs of affection for any adult who happens to be around.

It is important to seek parental guidance on how to respond to negative behavior from your adopted child. Parents who do best with special-needs adopted children are ones who are willing to be flexible, patient, and creative in managing unacceptable conduct. There are some situations that could arise when you are helping your child adjust that you may find hard to understand, such as if your child:

- Flinches when you try to hug her
- Gags or chokes when you feed her
- Soils herself, seemingly on purpose
- Is terrified of bath water

For children who were cared for in overcrowded orphanages, these behaviors are not uncommon. Talk with your pediatrician and mental health expert about how to cope with situations like these, should they arise.

Essential

You should find a family counselor who can help you, your spouse, and your other children as well as your new child. Such a counselor must be familiar with the unique attachment challenges in adoptions. If possible, get a referral from a friend or acquaintance who has adopted internationally, preferably from the same country as your child's.

You will get all sorts of advice from well-meaning people about how to raise your child; much of it may be helpful, but some of it could be useless or even harmful. In general, other parents or non-professionals do not really understand an international adoption until they have gone through one. If you have prepared yourself and your home, you can be hopeful that your family will flourish.

Integrating Your Child into the Family

Every child who comes into your family, whether by birth or adoption, changes the group dynamic. When you adopt, an only child may now have a sibling; instead of one gender, both may now be represented in your family. Adopting a child internationally also changes your family's culture.

Building and Strengthening Family Bonds

As indicated earlier, you can start the process as soon as you are matched with a child. Stay in touch as frequently as time zones allow. If possible, contact your child on a regular basis. Even if you just send photos, it will be something for your child to see. While you are waiting at home, start thinking and talking about your child as if he is part of your family already, so that all of you can begin to adjust. Talk with your children and spouse about the new child: "When Jin comes home, we can all play in the snow together" or "Next year there will be an extra stocking to hang on Christmas Eve!"

Bringing Your Child Home

When you finally have your visa to pick up your child, your travels may be stressful, but they will also become one of the most important periods of your life. Go prepared to collect and preserve as much about your time in the country as you can: take lots of pictures of the countryside where your child awaits you, including the orphanage or foster home and people he may have seen; buy a few souvenirs that he can cherish when he is older; make a special effort to photograph his caregivers and other children. When you return home, you could make a special scrapbook for him with all of these items in it.

 Fact

Your agency will let you know exactly what to bring when you go to get your child, but the list is certain to include gifts for your child's caretakers and possibly the other children at the home or orphanage, medicine in case she is ill, formula or fortified beverages, food, clothing, and toys.

You and your child may spend some time in a hotel room before leaving for the United States. This can be stressful for both of you, since you will both be in a strange place with strange people. These moments may be difficult, but they will be precious since they will be your first time alone together. By the time you arrive home after endless hours on airplanes, trains, buses, and cars, both you and your child will be tired and strained. Give yourself time to decompress and get used to each other. Your family and community may want to celebrate, but a celebration is not in the best interest of your child. Ask your family and friends to wait until your child is truly ready to be introduced to many new faces and voices. What you need most is time to develop a routine, become familiar with your child's way of communicating his needs, and rest. Your child needs your help in regulating his physical and emotional reactions to all the new stimuli in his world. This takes hours of quiet observation, close physical contact, and attentive responses that reassure him that you understand his needs and will help them be met in a loving and trustworthy way.

 Essential

If you'd like to understand the way your child feels, put yourself into this scenario: You wake up one morning to find that your house, neighborhood, and family have changed completely. Nobody speaks your language and they offer you food you don't recognize. They smile but you don't understand their gestures and they smell different. You aren't sure if they will hurt you or love you.

Plan to have several weeks, even months, off from work. Most international adoption experts recommend that one parent stay home with the child if possible, because attachment forms through physical connection and close emotional attunement. However, if that's not possible, be sure that you've lined up a consistent caregiver who will support your role and be with you for at least two years.

Your Child Will Need Time to Attach with You

Depending on your child's circumstances, you must rearrange your life to accommodate the new person in the family. Consider whether or not to enroll your child in school (if he is of school age) right away or to delay enrollment for several months or even a year after the adoption. You should make that decision based on your child's command of English, the attitude of school personnel, and his need for socialization. Often, a gradual introduction to his new life is the best plan. Many children adopted when older do much better in their overall adjustment if they are given time to learn basic language skills before entering the socially demanding environment of school.

The answers to questions about bonding and dealing with the impact of abuse or neglect are much more complicated. You must be sure that you have taken specialized training and that you are psychologically prepared to confront the very real challenges you will face. It won't be parenting as usual! See Chapters 14 and 16 for tips and more information.

If Things Fall Through

Most adoptions thrive, even international adoptions where so many variables are involved. But you should understand that sometimes your best intentions may not be enough. Circumstances beyond your control or expectations can arise. Sometimes a planned adoption does not work out, and sometimes you have to be the one to decide it is not working.

There are many reasons that an international adoption might fail, reasons ranging from you discovering that you weren't as well prepared as you thought you were to the child being much different from what you were led to believe to changes in local laws in the child's country that make the adoption impossible. Of all of these reasons, the most common one, by far, is that you were misled about the child's condition.

You may have gone through disappointments as you tried to conceive a child or have suffered miscarriage or loss, but when you decided to adopt you did so with your whole heart and you expected to succeed. You took the classes, bared your soul to social workers, and filled out endless forms designed to make you look closely at your reasons for adopting. You thought you'd considered every eventuality. Even though you have done everything you were supposed to, sometimes a situation is simply not one that will work for your family.

Example of a Failed International Adoption

While most international adoptions are successful and result in a close, bonded family, there are situations in which that is not possible. Too often, books about international adoption gloss over these possibilities. The following example is included because international adoptions can fail, through no fault of the adoptive parent.

Hilary and Bob were professionals with years of experience in child development—she was a behavioral psychologist and he a pediatrician. They already had two biological children, but felt a strong desire to parent a child who needed a home. After considerable research, including talking to friends who had adopted from Russia two years earlier, they hired the same facilitator and were matched to brothers, ages five and seven. Their initial visits and correspondence with the boys went very well, and they were told the children could come home to Ohio the last week in November.

The adoption was finalized in Russian courts on November 28, but trouble started when the new family drove from the village to Moscow for the flight home. Both boys erupted into volcanic tantrums, kicking, punching, and spitting as soon as they checked into their hotel. They broke furniture, even a window. Their behavior was dangerous and frightening. Only exhaustion stopped the frantic behavior; a few hours respite ensued and then the behavior started all over again.

After two days, the episodes seemed to diminish and there were periods of calm when the children clung to their parents. Then the ringing of the telephone or a siren blaring in the street started them screaming, running around the room, and thrashing away from Bob and Hilary's attempts to corral them.

Bob, who had been so caught up in the chaos that he couldn't think straight, realized that the older boy was displaying symptoms of sensory processing disorder. His behavior also indicated reactive attachment disorder and other neurological problems. The younger boy, on the other hand, seemed to be simply following his brother's lead.

HEARTBREAKING DECISIONS

At first, Bob and Hilary considered taking the younger boy home and hospitalizing the older one, but they soon realized that splitting up the children would lead to even more trauma. They discussed the situation with their social worker, who agreed that these children needed to be in a home where they would be the only children. Tearfully and with heavy hearts, they decided that the boys represented a greater risk than they were willing to take for their other children. With the cooperation of their social worker, attorney, and facilitator, they brought them back to the U.S. and helped them be readopted by another couple.

Hilary said, "At least we got them out of the orphanage and into a family where they're adjusting very well." She paused and her voice trembled, "But I feel so guilty, as if I should have known . . . or been stronger or something."

Finding Out the Information You Had Was Wrong

All of the information Bob and Hilary received indicated that the boys were emotionally and physically healthy enough to fit into their family. Although they knew they would have to deal with attachment issues, they didn't expect pathological behavior.

If you find yourself in a similar situation, it's pointless to beat yourself up. You know yourself and your family situation, and no matter how much you might want things to be different, you recognize when circumstances are beyond your control. The toddler who seemed well adjusted in the video and who came to you with seeming eagerness may have learned compliant conduct in order to survive in an environment where she had to compete with a dozen others. She may have serious emotional issues that won't surface until you take her away from the orphanage and the only life she knows. If you have requested an emotionally healthy child and been assured you have one, only to realize that she's emotionally damaged, you may not be able to parent her. Some parents might feel they have the right family for the situation, but it is important to know when a particular child is not a good match for your family. Being able to accept this possibility serves everyone's needs better than trying to make a situation work that will eventually end in a failed adoption or years of frustration and disappointment.

Grieving and Moving On

If this kind of situation should happen to you, the best thing for you to do is make the decision to end the adoption, before papers have been signed and the child's custody has actually been transferred to you. This is called a disrupted adoption, rather than a failed adoption, and it's easier, legally and emotionally, on everyone involved.

Whether the adoption is disrupted or failed, you need to get past it, and so does the child. First, you must acknowledge the reality of the situation, then you must give yourself space and time to mourn what might have been. While you mourn, however, remember that the child has lost much more than you, especially a child who has been abandoned, perhaps many times. You and the child will both need counseling and extended support.

Don't Give Up

It can be upsetting to consider a failed adoption, but you must remember that the vast majority of international adoptions are successful and have happy outcomes. You would not be entering into the situation in an educated way if you did not consider the possibility of a problem occurring.

It can also be very frustrating to decide you would like to adopt internationally, know that there are thousands of children in other countries who need homes, and then find that you have a very long wait to get a child. It can be tempting to give up at times.

Don't be afraid of taking the risks inherent in adopting internationally. True, you will probably have your patience tried over and over again and your emotional and financial resources may be strained, but if you want to be a parent more than anything else and if you are willing to dedicate your life to something much greater than yourself, you will find a joy beyond anything you can imagine. As successful adoptive parents attest, experiences that bring the most happiness are usually experiences that require the greatest effort.

CHAPTER 7

Adopting Through the Foster Care System

Like many people, you may find that adopting through state, county, or private foster/adopt agencies is a much simpler, less expensive way to add to your family. The foster care system is a rapidly evolving institution, with all the challenges inherent in a large bureaucracy. And it's not for the timid or uncertain. As with any adoption, your character and spiritual reserves will be tested beyond anything you may imagine; you'll struggle to work with people at various levels, many of whom may contradict each other. But foster care children desperately need homes, and by adopting a child in this way, you're doing something wonderful and positive that will make a tremendous difference in the life of a child.

Various Forms of Foster Care

The parents of children in foster care have lost temporary guardianship of their child to the state. Although permanent reunification or adoption must be the goal of foster care, children often go back and forth between foster homes and their families until they "age-out" of the system (turn eighteen and are considered adults). Children in foster care are not available for adoption until their parents' rights have been legally terminated and the child freed for adoption.

If you want to adopt through this system, you need to first understand the different categories of foster care and foster care adoption: temporary, long-term, foster/adopt care, and traditional adoption.

83

Temporary foster care refers to what most people think of as regular foster care. You provide a home for a child who has been removed from his parents. This could end up being a placement that lasts months or years, but the goal is always reunification. There are also foster homes that take emergency placements, which can be very temporary (a few days) until a more permanent foster home is located.

Long-term care involves special-needs children or sibling groups for whom adoptive homes just aren't available. These children remain permanently in a foster home or institutional home.

The foster/adopt category means the child is placed with a foster family that agrees to adopt the child if he becomes available for adoption. This is also called an at-risk placement, meaning the plan is for you to adopt, but that plan is at risk because the child may still be reunited with his parents. As a foster/adopt parent, you must enfold a child into your family, as if the placement were permanent, while you know it could be temporary. The child, however, must not feel temporary. This stability is most critical for infants and very young children. Older children also need reassurance that they are wanted and cherished.

A traditional adoption is also possible through the foster care system. You do not need to become a foster parent; you work with a state agency to find a child that is right for your family, and then you begin the adoption process. The child remains in his current foster home (although you do have contact) until the adoption is final.

Prepare Yourself Emotionally

Parents who seek to adopt through the foster care system are the true saints in the U.S. child welfare system. They place a child's needs above not only their convenience, but also their emotions. When you become a foster parent who is seeking to adopt, you can fall in love with a beautiful baby, a baby you want with every fiber of your being, a baby whom you're positive belongs with you. Yet your responsibility is to stand by and say goodbye to that child if she is reunited with her parents. As difficult as this is, you have the satisfaction of knowing you provided a stable home for a child who desperately needed one. Even though that child moves on, you have made a lasting impression on her.

 Essential

There is certainly nothing easy about being a foster parent or a foster/adopt parent. Those that do it do so because they deeply believe it is an important job that benefits everyone in our society, and that they're strong enough to do it.

If you are considering foster care or a foster care adoption, you must prepare yourself emotionally. There are no guarantees and you may become bonded to a child who will not be staying with you. If you are not sure if you would like to adopt a foster care child, you can first become a foster parent and experience what the system is like and what the children are like who are in it. This allows you to get your feet wet and make a difference without entering into a permanent arrangement.

Emotional Risks for Foster/Adopt Families

If you sign up to be licensed as foster/adopt, you agree to put yourself in an emotionally precarious position for the sake of children. Sometimes, the birth parents fulfill court-ordered requirements and are reunited with their children; however, a large proportion of those reunions fail. A child you are bonded to may be sent back to her original home, and it's also possible she will end up back in foster care again at a later date.

Another risk in foster/adopt situations is that a suitable biological family member will be found and the child will be removed from your home and placed there. This can happen even if you've had the child for a year or more. Although the Adoption and Safe Families Act of 1997 attempts to guarantee that children under five are "temporary" for no more than six to eight months (exact time varies by state), lack of sufficient personnel to conduct home studies and the fact that parents sometimes move to other states to try to find a friendlier judge all contribute to stretching out the time.

When considering the best interest of the child, some courts rule in favor of allowing the child to stay with the parent figure with whom the child has developed a trusting attachment, this frequently being the foster parents. It is important for foster/adopt parents to understand that this is not the norm or most common outcome of court rulings regarding permanent placement.

The Court of Appeals of Ohio affirmed a trial court's decision that awarded legal custody to foster parents rather than a qualified relative. The court held that considerations related to stability and continuity of care were overriding factors, even though both parties seeking legal custody appeared to be suitable custodians. This case is important because in general, relatives are given priority over foster parents, even when the foster parents have a deep bond with the child. In cases like these, the compelling factor is often not whether the foster parent or relative is more committed to the child, but whether the child has formed a secure attachment with the foster parent.

Licensing and Training

Because the fifty states have fifty different child and family services organizations, your first step should be to find out exactly how the system operates where you live. Learn what the laws are with respect to foster adoptions. If you are interested in foster/adopt, you will need to sign up for and take all the training your state and county offers. If you are pursuing traditional foster care adoption, classes may be available to you as well. If no one offers, be sure to ask.

Some states offer ten weeks of training, with classes held once or twice a week, usually in the evening. Others conduct the training in two or three full-time days. The classes are usually taught by a licensed social worker, with advanced degrees in behavioral sciences. Therapists, pediatricians, and experienced foster parents will often be called upon, too.

You will be taught about the realities faced by children and infants who come into foster care. You will learn about the different types of abuse and how children may feel about their biological parents. You'll also learn the signs of abuse and neglect and how these trigger reactions in children.

 **Alert!**

Red flags for potential abuse in infants and young children include failure to thrive—child doesn't meet average guidelines for growth and weight gain—and injuries inconsistent with age and activity, such as heavy soft-tissue bruising, broken bones, odd marks like circular burns, finger- or hand-print bruises, or cuts on buttocks, thighs, or calves.

You may find yourself tuning out during lectures because you think love will solve all problems, but children who have been removed from their families have serious emotional and physical issues. You need to pay close attention; you'll look back on the training and wish you had more. You won't experience every situation you learn about, but it is a good idea to be prepared with as much information as possible so you can handle any eventuality.

Learning about some of the abuse parents can inflict on their own children may infuriate or scare you, but you cannot let it discourage you from your desire to parent. With parental love, care, and dedicated commitment, most children can have a fulfilling and happy life.

Learning a New Paradigm

Whether you do a foster/adopt adoption or a traditional adoption from foster care, parenting a foster child requires you to set aside all your preconceived notions about parenting. Training will help you understand that standard discipline techniques probably won't work. For example, isolation or a time-out will frighten a child who was left alone by her parents.

When you adopt a child from foster care, you need to be prepared to deal with behaviors that you would not expect or have not seen in other children. Some of these behaviors can appear very irrational and confusing. It can seem strange to see a child do self-destructive things when she has been removed from an abusive home for her protection. Other behaviors, such as lying, stealing, or property destruction can be frustrating to foster parents who want to trust their foster child but find the child untrustworthy due to emotional problems. Not only must you be prepared to deal with it emotionally, you need to be prepared to seek out help for your child from doctors, therapists, tutors, and counselors. Finding out what assistance your child may need is half the battle; actually implementing that help is the other half. It can be hard to realize that you cannot provide everything your child needs, but remember, it would be unwise to take on this challenge unless you were willing to be flexible to meet your child's needs.

Preparing Your Family for a Child from Foster Care

Whether you have wanted to adopt all your life or you've recently decided that adopting a foster care child is a way in which you can positively shape society, know that your decision doesn't just involve you and your spouse or partner. You may have parents and other children who are affected by adding another person to the family, so be sure you're confident about the path you've chosen.

Explaining Your Decision to Other Children

Just how you explain your decision to adopt or foster/adopt to existing children will depend on the age of your child. In foster/adopt situations, you will need to explain to your children that you're going to be taking care of the new child because his parents are ill or can't take care of him right now. Younger children don't need more details than that. Talk to your older children with as much detail as is necessary for them to accept the child and feel safe. Remember that children have a tendency to see events in a very self-centered way. While you may foster several children before being able to adopt one, your other children need to know that they are permanent and not subject to being sent to another family.

If you are adopting from foster care, your explanations won't be much different than in any other adoption. This new child is becoming a member of the family because his birth parents could not care for him. Older children will want more details—such as why the parents can no longer care for the child or where they are.

 *Alert!*

Foster children can endure multiple losses (losing loved ones, a home, a school, best friends) within a short period of time, so their grief may be demonstrated in disconcerting ways. A foster child who has experienced frequent loss could bang his head against the floor, scratch himself until he bleeds, hide under the bed or in the closet, etc. Talk with experts about how to handle these behaviors.

Deciding to foster/adopt or adopt is very different from the decision to get pregnant. You probably wouldn't give your other children a vote on when you get pregnant, although they may tell you they want a brother or sister (or not). Since biology doesn't dictate, and you have a choice whether or not to adopt, you should involve all those who are old enough to have an opinion to participate in discussions about having a foster/adopt child in your home. After all, the new child will be a sibling. However, because it is impossible to guarantee a positive outcome to a child being placed in your home, your existing children should in no way feel responsible for the final placement decision. The final decision of having a new child in your home is an adult responsibility and children need to be free of that burden.

Reassuring Your Children

If you are planning to foster/adopt, prepare your children for the uncertainty of the situation, because they, too, will be sad if their sibling returns to his biological family. Depending on their ages, they may fear that they could be taken away from you, too. Take your children to training with you. If the rules don't allow them in the classes, share what you've learned when you come home—in the same way you would go over homework.

Tell them why you want to foster/adopt. For example, your situation may be like Manuel and Amy's who had five children ranging in age from eight to nineteen. They were called by Children's Protective Services in their state to take two-year-old Tyler. Manuel and Amy called a family meeting about what they could do for Tyler. You should hold the same kind of meeting if your children are old enough to have an opinion. Tell them generalities like "We've been asked to take a baby whose dad can't take care of him" and "Tyler will be with us at least three months (or whatever you've been told) because his dad is trying to turn his life around and get him back."

All of Manual and Amy's children enthusiastically accepted Tyler, thinking it would be six months or so before reunification. But Tyler's father continued using drugs, failed to comply with court-ordered parenting classes, and his parental rights were terminated. Manuel and Amy adopted Tyler after the other children proclaimed him their baby brother.

Understanding the Needs You May Face

If you choose to become licensed as a foster parent so you can pursue a foster/adopt adoption, you know that deep love for children in general is a prerequisite; however, the foster/adopt licensing process takes time, energy, and a great deal of patience. You may have high ideals and a positive mentality, but foster children need parents who can love unconditionally while setting reasonable boundaries and gently but firmly providing consequences when those boundaries are breached. This sort of parenting involves much training, experience, and flexibility, in addition to a whole lot of self-confidence. Experts call it "High Structure/High Nurture" parenting.

You may think you can't deal with an angry child who has neurological problems, but with training, you may surprise yourself. As an adoptive parent through the foster system, you choose burdens that most parents would never voluntarily take on. If you are clear on what you want from becoming a foster/adopt home or the adoptive home of a foster child, you will be able to accomplish a lot.

 *Fact*

Red flags for potential abuse in older children include frequent or oddly explained accidents, inappropriate touching of other children, and overt sexual behavior. Abused children can also be overly compliant, fearful, or restless, or profoundly disengaged from emotional interaction and affection.

Adopting a foster child who has repeatedly been hurt and or abandoned requires a stubborn patience and the ability to stand on a foundation of self-awareness and strong self-identity. With particularly damaged children, parents frequently find themselves losing not only their patience, but also their ability to empathize with their children. Additional training and therapeutic services are usually necessary for parents to maintain a sense of equilibrium while parenting a severely emotionally disturbed child. Listen to everything the counselors, social workers, and therapists tell you and be ready for anything.

Addressing Community Resistance to Foster Children

Many people have vague or negative views about foster children—the media perpetuates these negative perceptions. Lurid stories boost ratings and readership, but they're far from representing the truth about a significant portion of the population. Although there are exceptions, children come into foster care because of the behavior of their parents, not because of anything the children did. They may be damaged from untreated illnesses, exposure to drugs, neglect, and emotional abuse, but they're rarely a danger to the community.

Reactions from Extended Family and Friends

You may be offended or surprised by things family and friends say to you. People who care about you may be worried about your physical and emotional well-being. Try not to be upset if your mother says, "Are you sure you know what you're doing?" or your friend from work shakes his head and insists you're putting yourself "at risk."

 Essential

According to the American Academy of Child and Adolescent Psychology, African American children make up approximately two-thirds of the foster care population, and remain in foster care longer. Two out of three children who enter foster care are reunited with their birth parents within two years.

Also, remember that your loved ones haven't been inside your head as you pondered, prayed, and researched this significant step. Explain why you want to adopt through the foster care system. Invite your mother or friend to read some of the material from your trainings or recruitment brochures. Make the effort to reassure your loved ones, but don't let them deflect you from something your best instincts tell you to do.

Addressing Resistance

Deal with well-meaning but misinformed people by educating them. Keep your cool and make clear, informed statements. Emphasize that every adult has a responsibility to children in a society, and you have chosen to do your part. Very often, it is easy for someone to be opposed to a foster home in theory, but when they actually meet the parents who are making sacrifices for children and see the faces of children who have been put in this position, their feelings change. Becoming active in your community can help change public opinion.

Establishing a Flexible Mindset

Many experienced foster/adopt parents emphasize that you must be able to react quickly and to handle difficult situations. You must have mental and emotional toughness to respond to the realities of what's happening, rather than what you wish were true. You can't ignore behaviors in hopes they'll go away, and you must be perceptive about recognizing underlying reasons for disturbing conduct.

Understanding Your Child's Reality

Research reveals that children who are abused and neglected, especially during the critical early years, develop a skewed perception of the world due to complicated trauma. Their behaviors seem totally out of proportion to what's going on around them. That's because their internal reality, or what they believe about the world, and especially adults, is different from their current environment. They tend to displace rage about their mistreatment onto their adoptive parents.

Your five-year-old daughter, who arrived in your home starved with partially healed multiple fractures, may not recognize that she's now in a safe, nurturing place, because she responds to a set of expectations based upon multiple experiences of abuse in her past. Her life experiences have been filled with pain, and as her body heals and her emotions emerge from the blankness where she's been hiding them, she may stiffen and reject your gentle touch. She may hoard food under her bed, wander the house at night, and break or scratch furniture to relieve the high levels of anxiety and stored anger she has from her past.

It is difficult to predict what your child might do in reaction to her previous life, so you must remain flexible and prepared to deal with whatever comes your way with love and understanding. You can't truly know and understand what she has been through, but you can respond to her behavior with knowledgeable parenting skills and help her work through her situation. A good therapist, well versed in family dynamics and relationships, is a must for children who have suffered abuse.

Understanding Grief

Every child who is removed from a home suffers grief on some level—even infants who may not remember the situation when they are older. It is important for your child to process the grief she carries in order to become a whole, functioning person. Without moving through the developmental process of grief, she may get stuck at some point and be unable to move through grief to a final resolution.

The five stages of grief, as defined by author and activist Elizabeth Kubler Ross, are:

1. Denial or numbness
2. Protestation or overt anger
3. Sorrow and deep sadness
4. Hope that the pain will end
5. Acceptance of circumstances beyond one's control

As you support and guide your child through these stages, you will strengthen her attachment to you. Although grief is often explained as having stages, it is possible for your child to feel several stages at the same time or in a different order than another person. It is essential to allow your child to grieve, sometimes repeatedly, for aspects of her life and people that may not seem like losses to you, such as an abusive mother or a home without enough food.

Creating Routines and Family Time

A child who is recovering from a bad situation needs safety and reliability. As the foster or adoptive parent, you should create a solid family routine that creates a feeling of safety. Regular family time will help create attachment bonds.

Part of your routine should include eating at least one meal together every day as a family; sitting down at the table together is about much more than food. This is a time to share thoughts and feelings, to get to know one another a bit better. The circle of faces around the table creates an intimate community. When you have everybody in one place at one time, don't let the meal turn into a lecture or airing of grievances. Have a separate family council time to work through negative issues.

 Essential

If you are fostering, always refer to the child as "my daughter" not "my foster daughter." Your family and friends will know that Tammy is your foster child, and strangers have no need to know. However, understand that your foster child might not feel comfortable reciprocating by calling you "Mom" or "Dad." This can be an extremely difficult transition in a child's life, and it is best not to pressure her.

Besides meals, you should share pleasurable activities or outings. These don't have to be expensive. Walks around the neighborhood, picnics in the park, window shopping, story time at the library, and board or card games are all examples of bonding opportunities that don't cost anything. A weekly family game night is one routine you could institute.

Assign and track household chores. Knowing that he has a role in the family is important for your child, and giving him responsibility shows your faith in him. Set up regular bedtimes, with a simple routine that signals the end of the day. Wake your child at the same time each day. If he is school age, follow an after-school routine each day, such as snack, playtime, then homework. The more predictable your routine, the safer your child will feel.

One-on-One Time

In addition to family time, create opportunities for one-on-one activities with each child. Again, these opportunities don't need to be expensive. Let your child's interests guide you. If he likes sports, take him to a high school game or kick a ball back and forth in the backyard. Be especially careful not to waste interactive time with videos or television. When you do decide to watch a movie or program side by side on the couch, make sure that you're doing more than aimlessly flipping through channels. Pick out the movie or program together and talk about it afterward.

Staying in Control

All children want and need attention from the adults in their lives. Foster children may be adept at creating commotion and focusing attention on themselves through behaviors that can infuriate you. Keep in mind that, to a neglected child, even negative attention that feels under his control is better than being ignored. You are the adult, so don't be drawn into conflicts and arguments. It can be hard not to react emotionally, so you must always be thinking about what is happening and why and then search your mind for the most appropriate response.

Understand that when a foster child is placed in your home, he has lost everything familiar—his parents, neighbors, friends, pets, and so on. Everything changes, and while at his home of origin there may have been shouting, abuse, or deprivations, at least those things were familiar. Now, sounds, smells, and textures are different. A favorite blanket, shirt, or toy may have been forgotten or destroyed during the chaos of intervention and emergency placement. The loss of familiarity can be frightening; your job is to help build a new sense of familiarity in your own home.

Staying in control means that you must control your child's behavior and the environment. A routine is one important way to control both. You must also create clear rules of behavior and consequences and then calmly and rationally enforce these rules.

Recognizing When You're Losing Control

If you find yourself reacting negatively to your child or feel your anger escalating, give yourself a time out and leave the scene. You're human too, and you can't expect yourself to always feel calm and in control. Stepping into the next room and taking a few deep breaths can really give you some perspective on the situation. Then return, offering comfort, and when necessary, consequences, depending on the situation.

You should have a safe, neutral place where your young child can work through angry, chaotic feelings. Experienced parents recommend a soft, folding chair placed in the middle of the kitchen. Your child can sit out of range of walls or breakable objects, stamping his feet, yelling, crying, and waving his arms. While your child acts out the emotions he's feeling incapable of expressing in any other way, stay nearby; this is not a good time to isolate him.

Finding Support

As you know by now, you can't sit back and depend on others to care about your family as much as you do. Being an adoptive parent means that you're willing to do whatever it takes to make a family. Supportive families, friends, and communities make the process of adopting a child through social services much easier. The agency that conducted your licensing study or arranged your adoption should be able to put you in touch with others who have been or are in the same situation.

Question?

How can I stop rude, insulting behavior from my child?
You cannot control the words that come out of your child's mouth, you can only control your own behavior. When your child is using disrespectful language or behavior, tell him, "You must be really frustrated right now to use words like that, but that's not the way to get my attention. I'll talk with you when you're calm." If the unwanted behavior continues, you will want to be more and more disengaged so his misbehavior does not get additional attention.

Seek out state and national organizations. The National Foster Parent Association (NFPA) can direct you to local affiliates or people who will be able to answer your questions or help you form a group. Contact them on their Web site, *www.NFPAinc.org,* or by phone at 1-800-557-5238. You can also join local adoptive parent groups, where you are likely to find other parents who have adopted through foster care.

Be Creative

Don't wait for opportunities to come to you—take the initiative instead. Read through the bibliographies at the back of your training manual or materials. Call the local radio or TV station that interviewed a family with foster/adopt children and ask them to pass along your phone number.

The Internet has wonderful resources and, depending on where you live, can offer online chat rooms with foster/adopt parents, as well as direct you to a personal group.

 Essential

Try to utilize both Internet and personal groups. The Internet can bring a connection to hundreds of adoptive/foster parents and the anonymity can be liberating; but personal contact is valuable, too, because you'll gain strength from being face to face with people who understand your unique challenges.

Foster/adopt parents and parents who have done traditional foster care adoptions in your area can be your greatest resources. If nothing specific is in place in your town, take matters into your own hands and set something up. Reach out to your neighborhood and business community, arrange potluck suppers, play dates, and impromptu parades. Contact the local chamber of commerce to find companies that might be interested in supporting foster and adoptive parents by contributing seconds or outdated but usable items. You may be surprised by how cooperative and helpful people can be once they know a need exists.

Reach out to others who know how it feels to walk the same rough, often stony, path. You will be stretched to your limits, but your emotional and spiritual strength will increase, and you will join a select group who know the delight of realizing a broken child's heart has been mended.

CHAPTER 8

Adoption of Infants and Toddlers

Your paperwork has been accepted, and you've been notified that your child awaits you in a foster home, an orphanage in another country, or on her birth date at a hospital. If you've never been a parent before, you may be apprehensive, as well as unbelievably thrilled. You are about to embark on a wonderful adventure.

Bringing Your Child Home

The preparations you make will depend on whether your child is an infant (zero to twelve months) or toddler (thirteen to thirty-six months). A toddler is a baby in many ways, but has several unique needs and issues. An infant (at least until he starts crawling) stays where you put him for the most part, but a toddler will get into, on top of, and out of every piece of furniture and room in your house that you don't have barricaded or locked. Infants and toddlers have few language skills—they understand and communicate most things on an emotional level—but toddlers have greater difficulty in processing their emotions and regulating their behavior.

Infants

If you have been chosen by a birth mom to adopt her newborn, you may be able to be in the delivery room. You will most likely bring him home within a few days of his birth. If children's protective services has taken custody at the birth, your baby will be brought to you by a social worker or he will be placed in a foster home for a few days, depending on the laws in your particular state.

 **Fact**

Infants should have the opportunity to begin the attachment process immediately with a caregiver. Research indicates that even if a baby attaches to one person at birth, she is usually able to attach well to another loving person who steps into the parental role. As long as the caregivers don't change more than once or twice, a secure attachment will form with time.

The preparations you make and exactly what you do when you bring your baby home will depend on whether you're bringing him home from the hospital, a foster home, or an orphanage. In all cases, gather information so you know what you will face.

A newborn (up to about six weeks of age) who has had good prenatal care will be pretty much like a baby born to you. However, if his "womb life" was impacted by alcohol, drugs, or spousal abuse, he may already be physically and emotionally stressed or deeply affected. The good news is that he's hardwired, so to speak, to attach to his primary caregiver. If he's more than six weeks old but has been in a loving foster home, he may grieve for his foster mom (yes, babies grieve!), but the attachment should quickly shift to you.

You can expect normal infant behavior—crying, eating, pooping, and quietly absorbing his surroundings. If your baby became attached to another caregiver, you might find that his sleep patterns and appetite are disrupted or that he cries more. At this time, it is important to help him calm down by spending additional time holding, talking soothingly, stroking, and comforting him.

Toddlers

You might think adopting a toddler would be much easier than meeting the physical demands of an infant, or that you would have a better chance of building a relationship with a toddler than with an older child you adopt. However, you would be wrong in both instances. With an infant, the two of you can gradually get used to each other; infants sleep a great deal (at least in intervals), and feeding them is simple. Children older than toddler age have cognitive skills that help them process being adopted (they understand reason) and you can take them to therapy, which can make the process if not easy, at least not so difficult.

In comparison, keeping up with a toddler can drain your physical, as well as emotional, resources. Toddlers don't have the vocabulary to verbally express their anger and fear, and might push you away instead of accepting your love. It's important to talk to toddlers and explain things to them, but realize that they simply don't yet have the skills to understand everything you explain right now. Repetition will soon make your words familiar and comforting.

If your child is arriving from an orphanage, you will endure weeks or even months of waiting as the bureaucratic gears grind along. If you've been matched with an infant, he could grow into a toddler while you wait. Be sure that your agency keeps you updated with frequent pictures, so you can shift your thinking from "infant" to "toddler" if necessary.

Toddler behavior is unpredictable, even in a child who has been in one home since birth. Adoption can simply exacerbate some of the more difficult toddler behaviors—temper tantrums, sleeping difficulties, separation anxiety, throwing things, and testing limits. You will need to take your toddler's behavior one day at a time.

Setting Up a Nursery

Most new parents are excited at the prospect of setting up a nursery or room for the new child; it's a tangible sign that your child is on the way. What you need will depend, in part, on your child's needs. A child with special needs or who has been in an abusive home will have specialized needs, but in general, begin life with your newborn or neglected infant/toddler with the following items:

- A simple wardrobe that doesn't require you to pull anything over her head. Most infants hate the sensation and a frightened toddler won't enjoy it either. (The season of the year, how your house is heated or cooled, and whether or not you have a washer and dryer will determine exactly what clothing you buy.)
- A bassinette (for an infant) or crib with a firm mattress, fitted bottom sheet, and lightweight blankets
- An appropriate-size car seat with a bolster to keep your infant's head from rolling (a rolled receiving blanket will work)
- A child carrier (a front carrier works best for an infant)
- A changing table with open baskets underneath for storing clothing and diapers (a changing pad on top of a dresser works also)
- A baby bathtub
- Age-appropriate toys and books
- Feeding equipment such as bottles, spoons, bibs, and possibly a high chair
- Diapers and wipes
- Large receiving blankets for swaddling

While you do need a properly sized car seat, spend as much time as possible carrying your child around in a carrier/baby sling where she can hear your voice and feel your heartbeat. You may also want a swing or a vibrating infant holder, so you can put her down once in a while.

Extra Considerations for Toddlers
All of the above items are needed for toddlers, but there are some additional considerations. Your toddler may benefit from being

carried in a backpack if you have the physical strength. You'll definitely need a stroller, because an out of control toddler is practically impossible (not to mention quite heavy) to carry or drag.

Don't go to a great deal of expense or effort to decorate or buy lots of toys until you actually have your toddler in your home. Let her guide you toward what she needs and wants. Some children delight in merry-go-round, balloon, and clown room motifs and others are terrified of the bright colors and strange faces. It's best to have a bedroom that is calming and reassuring rather than garish and bright, as some children can be frightened by unfamiliar images and loud colors. When in doubt, go with white or beige walls and limit the room decorations at first. Don't fill a room with toys she will be unfamiliar with. A child who has been in a deprived situation does not benefit from overindulgence; introduce toys to her slowly and gradually.

Safety

Most experienced adoptive parents recommend that your baby sleep in your room for at least a month, and many parents wish to do so for even longer. Do, however, follow the advice of reliable medical and mental health professionals. Although cosleeping can be a way for you to start bonding to your baby, some pediatricians advise against it for newborns for safety concerns. If you don't want to sleep with your child in the same bed, but do want physical proximity, you can put her in a bassinette or something called a "side car" next to your bed. The idea is to be close enough to touch her and to hear her in the night, but avoid the possibility of rolling over onto her.

When your baby starts to roll over and scoot, usually at about five or six months, childproof your house. Put safety latches on your lower cabinets, cover electrical outlets, and attach gates across stairwells. Sit on the floor and look around. Check for hanging cords, tablecloths, wobbly lamps, or anything else that might be harmful if grabbed or mouthed by a curious baby.

Fact

The Apgar test, (Activity, Pulse, Grimace, Appearance, and Respiration), done immediately after birth, rates a newborn's physical condition on a scale of zero to ten. Babies with an average score of seven are considered healthy. Knowing your baby or toddler's score is a very useful piece of information; it can alert you to whether your baby might benefit from concentrated early childhood stimulation to activate healthy brain and neurological development.

Plan to Take Care of Yourself

Sleepless nights and struggles with a fretting, upset, or sick infant or toddler will be your new reality. A new young child in the house will upset everybody's routine. If you aren't careful to eat a healthy diet, get sufficient sleep, and exercise, your body won't be able to meet the extraordinary demands.

Although you are thrilled to welcome a new member of the family and are trying to be a perfect parent, step back and be realistic. Remember that you can't be a perfect mom or dad, because nobody can. Parents don't come in "perfect."

Essential

Experienced parents recommend you secure the sleep you need by sleeping and getting up at the same time every day, even on weekends; using your child's sleepy-time rituals for yourself as well; making your bedroom a place for rest and rejuvenation; getting enough exercise; and establishing a restful daily quiet time for yourself during your child's naps.

The first month home will be the most difficult because your child will need your consistent presence. Call on your support network to relieve you for an hour or two at your house when needed. Go into your bedroom and take a nap or read a book. Relax in a bubble bath and listen to music—do whatever you enjoy.

All experienced adoptive parents stress that you must establish a schedule as quickly as possible. The more continuity your child encounters, the more he will begin to trust you. Meal and bedtimes should be regular, although don't be so rigid that you fail to respond to his needs quickly. Remember that you aren't spoiling him when you answer his cries with food, a diaper change, or a cuddle.

Bonding Techniques for Babies

Babies change rapidly physically, and are born with billions of brain neurons that go through connection and pruning processes as babies experience life and interact with their environments. Repeated experience wires a child's brain. Each time your baby tries to touch her butterfly mobile or reach toward your face, tiny bursts of electricity knit neurons together. She needs recurring, consistent activities that stimulate the various centers of her brain. If her previous environment was sterile or abusive, she won't have developed as many pathways allowing her to learn.

Revising Your Baby's First Experiences

Babies under four months old attach more quickly with their caregivers than older babies—if they've had secure, reliable nurturing from the moment of birth. If your baby has come from foster care or an orphanage and you suspect a lack of attachment, recreate, as much as possible, the first weeks of life for her with a more positive experience.

Hold your child and swaddle her. Some moms who've been there recommend that you do at least one feeding while kangarooing—holding her against your bare chest, naked except for a diaper. Warm milk, if you aren't breastfeeding, the sound of your voice, and the softness of your body all signal to your baby that she is secure and her needs will be met.

Feeding

You and your baby communicate during feeding times. Your baby feels hunger pangs and cries. She sucks on her fist or blanket and cries again. Then you pick her up and hold her close. Warm milk quiets the hunger pangs, your scent and touch become entwined with sensations of hunger going away, and the eye contact you make work together to foster attachment. It is important to make feeding time with your baby an intimate time, removed as much as possible from distractions and abrasive sounds. Turn off your cell phone, television, and computer. Focus your attention on your baby and watch her closely. This will help you learn her unique way of communicating her needs, making feeding a mutually gratifying experience for both of you.

 **Question?**

Is it possible to breastfeed my baby?
Yes, more and more moms are breastfeeding their adopted infants. The process takes preparation with medication and or pumping, and almost always needs supplementation with formula. But it is possible, especially if you've breastfed before. Contact the La Leche League International at *www.llli.org* and discuss the specifics with your doctor.

Avoid watching TV or feeding your baby in the middle of any commotion. If you have visitors during feeding time, go into another room where you will not be distracted. This is especially important during her first few weeks at home. It's fine to have visitors, but keep their visits brief during the initial weeks, and be sure you and your partner are the main ones feeding your baby.

If you have other children, try to feed her alone in the beginning, gradually shifting to become a general part of the family at feeding times.

Alert!

> After your initial adjustment period, when you need to leave your baby for a while, give her something that smells like you, like a pillow case or T-shirt. Several moms recommend making a small blanket out of flannel and sleeping with it before you have to leave.

If your child was born with alcohol or drugs in her system, she may be hypersensitive to being held. She may arch her back and turn away from you, and this can make feeding difficult. Experienced parents suggest that you lie down beside your baby on the floor when you give a bottle. Prop her so she's on her side and you can hold the bottle while she looks into your eyes. Lightly touch her hair or hand, then gradually increase your strokes or patting. If your child consistently rejects your touch, however, have her evaluated by a pediatric neurologist and/or a sensory integration specialist.

Playing

Don't take parenting so seriously that you fail to engage your child in silliness and having fun together. Make faces and stick out your tongue, mimic your child's gestures and sounds. Your child will quickly figure out that language is a two-way process. The more you respond to babbles, coos, and smiles, the more your baby's brain will make the connections between words and what they mean.

Babies love the game of peek-a-boo; you may get your first belly laugh through this game of hiding your face behind a blanket or pillow and popping out with a big smile and "Peek-a-boo!" This is more than a game; your child is learning that just because she can't see something, it hasn't disappeared. She's learning to trust that you will always come back.

 Fact

Play with your child as he tolerates and enjoys the activity. If your baby turns away from you, he's probably tired or overwhelmed. Give him space, but use your intuition to be sure that you aren't allowing him to disengage from you and retreat into where he was before you brought him home.

As your baby gains control over her body, interact with her physically. Play patty-cake and patty-feet. Hold her weight in your hands and bounce her up and down. Touch her nose, mouth, and ears while you name the part, then take her hand and say the words while she touches your nose, mouth, and ears. This kind of touching will help her feel physically comfortable with you.

Bonding Techniques for Toddlers

The dividing line between babies and toddlers is vague; usually, a baby is considered a toddler once he walks or is one year old. There are distinct characteristics that make a child a toddler. All toddlers tussle with lack of language to identify and deal with their emotions; adopted toddlers may face tremendous challenges and act out their feelings.

Your toddler's body and physical skills outstrip his cognitive abilities; he won't be able to resist climbing up the bookcase or running into the street. You won't be able to take your eyes off him for more than thirty seconds, and then only if you're in the middle of an enclosed play area or if he's asleep in his crib.

Toddlers' Needs

Your newly adopted toddler's needs will depend on his developmental age and whether or not he came into your home from a nurturing foster home, an orphanage, or perhaps the streets of a third-world country. Toddlers whose lives have been disrupted multiple times or who come from a very different culture will need specialized help to learn they are safe with you.

Many of the techniques recommended in this chapter for use with a baby will be appropriate for your toddler, such as being wrapped in a soft, wooly blanket, smiling eye contact, and finger plays, as long as you pay attention to his body language. Nothing you do should ever be forced, painful, or demeaning.

Remember that you are forming attachments and establishing yourself as the loving, dependable adult in your child's life. Some disciplinary tactics simply won't work for toddlers with attachment issues. Be sure that you are involved with a knowledgeable professional and a support group who will help guide you; most of all, realize that toddlers with attachment issues can behave very differently than children who have had the benefit of forming a secure attachment from birth. Seeking help may be essential for meeting your toddler's attachment needs effectively.

Food

As with babies, food is the main vehicle for building attachment with a newly adopted toddler. Your toddler may not have been fed adequately previously and may not be able to recognize his hunger. He needs to know that you, his parent, will consistently provide food. Try to get some information about what he was fed before, so that you can introduce new foods gradually.

Some parents have successfully built trust and attachment by regressing their toddlers to a bottle feeding once a day. In her book *Toddler Adoption*, Mary Hopkins-Best details how to use food and bottle feeding to facilitate attachment and heal the misperceptions about the world and wounded places in your child's heart.

If your child is coming from another culture, learn to prepare simple foods and beverages that will be familiar to him. If your child is coming from a foster home, meet with the foster parents and find out his likes and dislikes.

Sleep

Sleep is also important for a toddler. Ask questions about his sleeping habits if possible: Did he sleep alone? With another child? In a room with many children? What rituals surrounded sleeping and waking up? Many parents use the family bed to help their toddler attach more securely, or the modification of a "side car" bed or mattress on the floor beside the parents' bed.

Some toddlers will go through a honeymoon period where they go off to bed without needing much help from you and sleep through the night, because they've been conditioned to do so by the orphanage they came from. Mary and George told friends that their two-year-old daughter adopted from China went to bed without any fuss and slept through the night. They thought she was admirably independent, not realizing that she was behaving as she had at the orphanage and was disconnecting from them. A child in this situation may later develop problems sleeping once she becomes completely familiar with her surroundings.

 Essential

Famous adoptees include Johann Sebastian Bach, Nancy Reagan, Truman Capote, Nelson Mandela, George Washington Carver, Ted Danson, Jesse Jackson, Faith Hill, Gerald Ford, John Lennon, Moses, Eleanor Roosevelt, Seal, Malcolm X, and all Dalai Lamas.

You should develop a simple, loving bedtime routine for your toddler that fits your family's style and situation. Common rituals involve a warm bath and a foot, back, or hand massage; tooth brushing; toileting or diapering; and a story and/or song. Whatever you do, make sure it's relaxing and involves comfortable physical interactions. Also, keep the time under control, because children will add and embellish, and you may find yourself spending two hours doing what should only take thirty minutes at most. In addition, if you have a spouse or partner, alternate who puts the child to bed, so that each of you has the same opportunity, and so your child forms attachments to both of you.

Dealing with Toddler Behavior

Your preverbal toddler will experience grief, loneliness, and fear that he may express in screaming tantrums or whining, clinging behavior. How you deal with these emotions will set the tone for your relationship for the rest of your lives. Above all, stay calm, especially when he's out of control. If he whines and is impossible to pry off your leg, give him a few minutes of reassuring cuddles as you repeat how much you love him. He'll be able to separate from you when he's ready.

Toddlers need a parent who provides consistency. Don't allow him to pull the dog's tail today and then discipline him for the same thing tomorrow. While it is true that your toddler is going to have a hard time adjusting to the adoption, that does not mean you should permit behavior that you find unacceptable. It does mean you need to be understanding about why that behavior is occurring and think creatively about how to stop or redirect it.

Acknowledge his past and shower him with extra affection, but have clear boundaries that demonstrate that you are in charge and he no longer has to be hypervigilant or worried about what will happen next. Older babies and toddlers will not have words to process their feelings, but their bodies remember where they have been and their brains will react. Use simple words to express your love and happiness in being his mom (or dad). If he pulls away from you, he's telling you that he's never experienced appropriate nurturing from an adult and is frightened. So stay close, but don't force the issue.

Addressing the Adoption

Your baby or toddler doesn't have language skills, but just because she can't communicate how she feels in words doesn't mean she's unaffected by what's happening to her. Your preverbal child processes her environment emotionally and physically; you can read what she's feeling by watching her actions and emotions. Give simple explanations and descriptions as you care for her. She may not be able to comprehend everything you are explaining now, but with time she will, and since you started talking about it from the moment she arrived, it will always be part of her history and understanding of her own life. By the time she is three, she will be able to more fully comprehend your explanations.

Recognizing the Important People from Your Child's Past

The people who cared for your child before she came to your family are important to her. This could include her birth parents, foster parents, foster siblings, caregivers in an orphanage, or even other children in an orphanage. Separating from these people will be traumatic. There may have been neglect, even abuse, but the experience was your child's only reality. Ignoring or dismissing it will not make it any less real.

Alert!

Don't let your child disengage and shut you out. Initiate eye contact and light touch. If she runs away, go after her. However, don't move suddenly or grab your toddler, because such actions may trigger memories of being hurt by those she lived with.

Spend a few minutes on a regular basis looking at pictures of people and places from her past and talking about where she was and how she came to be with you. Emphasize how happy you are that she is with you and that she will stay there. As she sees the pictures and hears your descriptions, she will begin to comprehend the changes in her life on a mental, rather than physical, level.

Talk about the Adoption

From the time your child first comes home, tell her the story of her adoption. Describe your waiting, and your delight when the referral or match actually came. Weave a story with your child about where she came from, with herself and orphanage or agency personnel as central characters. Tell about the day the adoption was finalized in court, when a judge said "You are now a forever family."

Remember that there are details of the adoption that will not be appropriate to share until your child is older. For now, keep your explanations simple and calming.

Remain Reassuring

Acknowledge ambivalent feelings your child may have, but always express your certainty that you belong together and will never be separated. Some parents use their religion or belief in a higher power to reinforce the rightness of their families with statements like, "God chose you for us."

Important Recordkeeping Tips

As soon as you have a referral, clean up and organize the stacks of papers and forms you've used in your search. Then start collecting information and writing in your journal, recording names, places, and dates. Don't forget to include agency personnel and your interactions with them. Take notes when you talk to social workers, lawyers, and others. Some of this collecting may be disheartening if the referral falls through, but it's important to preserve as much as you can. Also, these details will be the basis of your child's personal story.

Documenting Milestones and Life Events

If your baby comes home from the hospital with you, your recordkeeping will be similar to that for any infant. Clip newspaper headlines, take pictures of the hospital, or put the ID bracelet in an envelope. As your child grows up, take lots of pictures and jot down why you took them, with your perspective on how the moment unfolded. Track your child's developmental and emotional milestones in a journal or baby book.

You should also keep as much information as you can about the birth parents and extended family, even if yours is a closed adoption. This kind of information is not appropriate to share with your child now, but will be useful in later years. Just the fact that you're keeping it emphasizes your commitment to your child.

Find the Time to Preserve the Moments

If your baby comes to you after months or even years in a foster home or institution, compiling a life book becomes more critical. Your agency should help you with the data collection. Include copies of medical records and court reports. If you don't have photographs, create word pictures that you can use later when your child is older to help him understand his roots.

You may only have time to toss your pictures and notes into big envelopes, but try to take a half-hour weekly to make notes, take photos, or label photos. Otherwise, your little one just might grow up before you know it, and you will have lost the moments.

CHAPTER 9

Adoption of Preschool Children

Adopted preschool children can have behaviors, issues, and concerns similar to those of toddlers, depending on their developmental ages and experiences. If your child is over three years old, he will be considered a preschooler, but you may, especially during his first weeks or months with you, have to treat him as you would a toddler or infant (see Chapter 8). If he received adequate, loving care, he will attach to you more quickly. But if he was abused or abandoned, you may be in for a struggle and will need to recreate the nurturing infancy he may have missed.

Preparing Before the Placement

As with infants and toddlers, you can do much to prepare for your preschool child before she comes home to you. If your child is coming from a loving foster home, she will still need to adjust to the adoption and to you, and this will take time, patience, and understanding. If your child had years of neglectful or abusive parenting, she probably will have attachment issues and will have learned that she cannot trust anyone but herself. Your job will be a balancing act between being the consistent, loving adult who meets her needs and being the in-charge adult who keeps her safe and disciplines her when necessary. A large part of your work will involve understanding why your child behaves as she does and stopping her rejection of you that interferes with building attachment.

Understanding Emotional Needs

As you prepare yourself mentally for your child to come home, you must understand where she is, developmentally. The preschool period is a time of tremendous intellectual and emotional growth. Under normal circumstances, children of this age develop vocabularies that reflect their ability to understand cause and effect, past, present, and future. They also learn to delay gratification. If your child is being adopted from foster care, there should be medical records available that will help you understand exactly where she is in her development and what progress she needs to make. Take some time to learn about child development and talk with your pediatrician about ways that you can help her development.

 **Alert!**

If your child didn't get good care consistently before coming to you, she will likely be physically delayed. You may be amazed at how dramatically your three- or four-year-old gains pounds and inches within a few months of receiving proper nutrition and love in your home. Your pediatrician can offer advice and guidelines throughout this experience.

Your child's life until now was probably not normal. Depending on her experiences, she may need therapy and or medication. Most of all, she needs consistent, involved parenting that will take a lot of energy on your part. Although she shouldn't be in situations that would take her away from you for extended periods, she should have an opportunity to play with other children on a regular basis.

Preparing Your Home

Your new child will need her own personal space that should include a bed, a chest of drawers, and part of a closet. She shouldn't have her own room, unless she's your only child or her only sibling is a boy. A possible exception to this is if your child has had a history of sexual abuse or acting-out behavior that has been sexual in some way. If this is the situation, then it is best for your child to have a private bedroom where she will not be able to inappropriately act out sexually with other children in the family. If she does have her own room, it should be very near yours.

The personal space you develop for her shouldn't be a place where she can easily detach or withdraw from the family. Use neutral, soothing colors that can be transformed as she grows up. Wait until she's been in your home for a while before you invest in something special like a canopy or racecar bed. It's best to start slowly and build a child's room according to her interests and needs. Remember that a child who has come from a very sparse existence may be easily overwhelmed by an overdecorated room.

Use Your Waiting Time Wisely

If your child waits in an orphanage or overseas foster care, a great deal of time can elapse before you will be able to bring her home. Most parents describe this period as agonizing, but it can also be productive. Use the time to get to know your child through pictures, videos, and computerized satellite phones when possible. As a preschooler, she's developing language and cognitive skills that can enhance the bonding process.

Start to create a life book that you can give your child when she arrives. This book should have sturdy pages and be able to withstand frequent handling. It should contain pictures of you and your spouse or partner, other children in the family, pets, neighbors, main areas in your town, plus the outside and inside of your house. It should have pages already set up where your child's mementos and pictures from her past can be posted if you have any.

Many foster parents keep a life book like this for each foster child and send it along with them when they return to their biological homes or go to another placement. Copies of it are often kept with social services, in case it gets lost or destroyed along the way, so if your child comes to you from another foster home, she may arrive with a life book already in progress, which you can then add to once she arrives and becomes part of your family.

If Your Child Starts Acting Out

Your child, may spend his first few days or weeks with you displaying his best behavior, especially if being compliant or "the good child" brought him attention and food in his birth home. The length of this honeymoon varies, but as soon as he's comfortable, he'll probably start testing you to see if you really can be trusted and relied upon to provide consistent, loving rules and a safe, permanent home.

Preschoolers, especially those from emotionally impoverished backgrounds, have limited vocabularies and cognitive abilities with which to make sense of their world. Your child may exhibit rage, depression, and a host of other emotions and reactions that he can't adequately explain or express. Until now, he may have had to rely on himself or have had to take care of the adults in his life. Depending on what his life was like before he joined your family, he may have learned to dig food out of the garbage or to pull a blanket over and tiptoe around a passed-out parent, and thought such behaviors to be normal and expected.

When he is thrown into the new environment of your home, those old behaviors will no longer work for him and he will be scrambling to determine how to behave. Your child may wonder just how bad he can be before you reach your emotional limits. He may soil himself, break things, run away or hide, and other unacceptable behavior. But the worse he acts, the more he needs to be reminded that he's loved and really home. Acting out is a defense mechanism against the pain of being ignored, left behind, or rejected. If your preschool-aged child has an abuse/neglect history, understand that many of his behaviors will be driven by fear; fear of not having enough food, fear of being rejected or punished harshly, fear of losing a nice place to live and a loving family through no comprehensible reason.

Teaching the Basics

In addition to trying your patience, your child may have no understanding of his physical needs. You may have to teach such basics as putting on a sweater when it's chilly, how often to bathe, how to use utensils to eat, and so on. A child who has always been cold, hungry, and untouched will need you to demonstrate that you can and will protect him. When you help him with these needs, talk about them. You could say something like, "Devon, I see you shivering, so I'm going to give you a sweater because it doesn't feel nice when you're cold. I love you and don't want you to feel cold," as you help him slip his arms into the sleeves. He will learn to trust you, that you know things he doesn't, and that he can rely on you to provide what he needs.

 Essential

Famous adoptive parents include Madonna, Al Roker, Angelina Jolie, Calista Flockhart, Magic Johnson, Oscar de la Renta, Ronald Reagan, Rosie O'Donnell, John McCain, Stephen Speilberg, Tom Cruise, Walt Disney, Ozzy Osbourne, Erma Bombeck, Jane Fonda, Hugh Jackman, Roy Rogers, and Meg Ryan.

Adults in your child's life may have disappointed him again and again, as well as hurt him physically and emotionally. Teaching him to trust you may be difficult because he may pull away, indulge in raging tantrums, and other attempts to exert control. He learned these behaviors because they helped him to survive the environment he was in. With patience, you can help him understand that he can trust you and that trust can form the basis of his new life.

Help Your Child Change Negative Behavior

If your child developed negative behaviors as a coping mechanism at his previous home, it is up to you to show your child that these don't work and aren't needed in your home. This demonstration will require you to stay in control and react neutrally to rages and tantrums. Your priorities are to keep your child safe and redirect the part of his brain that prompts the behavior. As odd as it may sound, if your child erupts into volcanic anger, he may be feeling safe enough with you to express his fear and conflicting emotions. He may never have been safe enough to express himself in this way.

 Fact

Children who have been physically or sexually abused should never be forced into a hug or held tightly when they are out of control. Instead, a child like this should be directed to sit in a chair in an open space. Gently sit her down when she jumps up, even if you must do so every ten seconds.

If your child does have angry outbursts, try to figure out what prompted the rage. One possible explanation is overstimulation. Grocery shopping, unexpected visitors, videos, music, and a host of other innocuous things may be too much for a preschooler from a deprived situation to process within the first few months of being in your home. If overstimulation seems to be the trigger, take him into a quiet room where you can dim the lights and sit with him. Depending on what you know about his previous experiences, either hold his hand or gently rock him. This quiet calming behavior will reduce the overstimulation and allow him to become calm and relaxed.

Establish Simple Boundaries

Your preschool child needs to understand, on a basic level, that you are in control and that you can set and enforce boundaries. Small children instinctively know that they are too small and weak to take charge of their lives. When the adults who care for them fail to set up parameters for behavior, children become anxious and afraid.

That anxiety and fear will be expressed through tantrums, running away, and defiance.

You, not your child, should decide what and when the family eats, when people go to bed, and other basic lifestyle issues. Set up a regular schedule for daily activities, a schedule that doesn't vary from day to day. Children from chaotic backgrounds need the assurance that things will be the same tomorrow.

Award Appropriate Consequences

Consequences should be immediate and relate directly to the misbehavior. For example, if you have a no-hitting or no name-calling rule in your home and your child hits or screams vile names at you, you must stop the hitting and screaming. Do so in a gentle, calm way and take your child to a specific place you have set up. Put one minute per year of age onto a timer and sit nearby. If your child continues to scream and thrash about, stop the timer and say, "Your time will start when you are calm and in control." Reiterate why he is in his "mad" place and what you are doing to help him redirect his behavior.

At first, you may have to start and stop the timer several times, but if you persist and stay calm and loving, he will eventually realize that he can't control you with his anger.

Calming Preschoolers' Common Fears

If your preschooler has come to you from a loving foster home and has no memory of a bad home, she will likely experience normal preschooler-type fears, which may be exacerbated because of the newness of the situation. Fears of the dark, unknown people, or things like clowns or monsters are normal fears, but a child who is being moved to a new home is likely to experience these kinds of fears on a deeper level.

A newly adopted preschooler from a difficult background is likely to commonly fear not having enough to eat and being hurt by those who should care for and love her. She needs to develop what

Dr. Karyn Purvis, director of Texas Christian University's Institute of Child Development, and her team describe as "felt safety." You know that your child will have enough to eat and will be safe in your home. You know that you would never hurt her in any way, but she doesn't know this. If she is from a deprived situation, every adult in her life may have disappointed her.

Calming the Fear of Hunger

Hoarding food or overeating to the point of vomiting are indications that your child was fed randomly and never enough. If you find rotting food hidden in your child's dresser drawer, you may be disgusted or horrified by the smell. But scolding won't help her understand that she doesn't need to save up against starvation. Instead, acknowledge that people may have neglected her and deprived her of food, but that you are her parent and your job is to be sure her tummy is full and her body nourished. Along with the acknowledgment, give her granola bars or other nonperishable food to keep handy. You may also need to institute a plan to keep the kitchen off limits, such as locking the door.

Eating so much that she vomits is another way your child may hoard food. She's desperate to make sure she stuffs enough in so she won't suffer hunger pangs for awhile. She has also lost touch with her body's signals that she's full, and you must gently and consistently give her the right food in the right amounts. Portion control is key. Your pediatrician should be your guide in making sure she receives appropriate nourishment.

Calming the Fear That Keeps Her Awake

Your child may wander the house at night and be unable to sit still for any length of time. She may be simply reacting to being in a new and strange environment or grieving her lost home. But if she's from an abusive situation, her body is caught up in a fight-or-flight reaction where her brain chemistry is actually telling her she's in danger. Even when the environment is safe, she's on high alert. She probably never knew when she would be attacked verbally or physically, so now, she can't shut down or relax.

As with food, you must model appropriate behavior and establish a regular sleep schedule. Night-time rituals signal to your child that she's in a safe place, that she can unwind and doesn't have to be vigilant. If you find her up in the night, gently put her back to bed and take a few minutes to calm her. You may have to do this again and again. She will learn to trust that you can and will protect her.

Reducing the Fear of Trust

If your child stiffens when you reach out to her and turns away from hugs or other displays of affection, she was likely hurt by those who should have nurtured her. She may never have learned how to process touch and cannot tell the difference between a gentle pat and abuse. If you think that she has dysfunction of sensory integration, the more quickly you deal with it, the more peaceful your home will be. Consult your pediatrician and therapist. However, be aware that the field of sensory integration is still not fully understood or recognized by all pediatricians and therapists.

You can use simple techniques to teach your child to accept your touch. Always approach her from the front—never come up behind her or move suddenly when you are near her. Crouch down to her level or sit beside her when you talk to her or interact with her. Use one finger to lift her chin and initiate eye contact. Say things like, "Let me see your eyes" or "I can see my smile reflected in your eyes."

 Essential

Show your child how to identify safe people in her life. Tell her that safe people are kind and don't threaten her or try to make her keep secrets from you. Tell her that if she ever feels funny or uncomfortable in the presence of any adult, to immediately come to you, even if the person smiles and seems to be friendly.

Although your child may push you away emotionally, don't leave her alone either physically or emotionally. Encourage her to use words to express her feelings and work with her to identify those feelings. Pursue your child, rather than letting her close you out. If your child has serious problems, you and your family will need the help of your support system.

Meeting Your Preschooler's Unique Challenges

Your child may have lost several primary caregivers and need the security of full-time parenting, especially if he's been through a failed adoption or multiple foster care placements. In such cases, many adoption professionals recommend that you or your partner put career plans on hold and be a full-time parent for at least a year. If you're single or can't take time away from your career, you'll need extra support. You must understand the feelings and perspective of your child that exist under negative behaviors, and be able to be loving and nurturing as you become the safe, capable adult for a child who is not able to trust.

Deflect Detaching Behaviors

Don't be fooled by a child who displays inappropriately mature behavior, such as putting himself to bed without your help or making his own food. Many children, especially those from crowded orphanages or deficient homes, have never had anyone to do those things for them. They may also not demand your attention during the day and wander off to entertain themselves, thereby avoiding interactions with you.

Don't allow your child to spend too much time alone without you or your support person's involvement during the first months of placement. Many adoption professionals estimate that you will have to actively work on promoting attachment for at least a year for every year of the child's age before he came to you. It is only through spending time with you that your child will be able to adjust to the adoption.

The Need for Professional Therapy

If you can't coax your child into interactions and he continually rejects your gentle offers of affection, don't wait until you are ready to give up. Consult with a therapist who is experienced and trained in attachment issues.

Another indication of the need for professional intervention is angry outbursts that are out of proportion to the precipitating event. For example, you ask your child to pick up scattered toys and he launches into a screeching fit, complete with kicking and fist pounding. Other indications include cruelty to animals, setting fires, stealing, and hoarding food after you've provided nonperishable items for him to keep.

Take heart in the knowledge that medical tools exist today that didn't only a few years ago. Magnetic resonating instruments (MRI), sonograms, and other noninvasive procedures have revolutionized brain research. If necessary, doctors can watch your child's brain in action and pinpoint the behavioral programs, medicines, and special diets that will foster regrowth of neurons and strengthen areas of weakness in his brain. This can lead to better behavioral self-control and mood stability.

Controlling the Environment

Your child may be disobedient, insist on being left alone, or aggressive toward others. Because your child is a preschooler, you can control his environment. Be careful about putting him into situations where he's liable to act out. For his first few months in your home, stay away from crowds or shopping malls. Too many people and too much stimulation will overload his ability to cope (note that overstimulation can be a problem for all children, adopted or not, of all ages).

Since you can't protect him forever, gradually introduce social situations that allow him to practice skills he'll need to enter and succeed in school.

Understand and Respect Your Child's History

One of the hardest things for you to deal with may be the fact that your preschooler's life didn't start when you met her. Not only did you not give birth to her, but years elapsed before you became a family. During those years, she may have failed to receive adequate nourishment for both her body and spirit. Without stimulation and critical nutrients, her brain didn't develop normally, and her growth was delayed. You will grieve that you couldn't provide the safe home, appropriate care, medical treatment, healthy meals, and quiet, safe place to rest that she needed then. Nothing you do or say will erase her formative years or give back what was taken away. However, the power to change and shape her future to be more positive and life affirming is directly in your hands.

Respect that reality and reassure your child that her story's newest chapter begins with you and will continue forever. Be as nonjudgmental as possible when she asks you questions or starts to talk about what happened to her. Tell her that she has the right to talk or not to talk about certain times in her life and that you will always listen and help her understand things. As she opens up and you listen, interject your sympathy while expressing your sorrow and support.

 **Question?**

When my friends want to know the gory details about my daughter's life in a Russian orphanage, what do I say?
If your friends interact with your child on a regular basis, give the bare essentials: "Tara was one of twenty children three to four years old who had the same caregiver, so she's learned to throw tantrums to get attention." Otherwise, say something like, "Tara's story is hers, and I'm not comfortable giving many details."

Important Recordkeeping Tips

Your preschooler may not remember every placement or caregiver he has had, but he at least remembers where he came from immediately before coming into your home, so it is important that you acknowledge the reality of his previous life. In doing so, you validate him and demonstrate that you, his new parent/s, are committed to building continuity and forging eternal bonds. You show him that you accept everything about him. You must actively seek out areas where you can get information. If you adopted him from another country, you may have difficulty reconstructing his past because of language and cultural differences.

Find Out about Previous Experiences

When possible, contact biological grandparents, older siblings, uncles and aunts, and foster parents—anyone with whom your child interacted. Collect anecdotes and descriptions of him as a baby and toddler. Try to find pictures to build his life book. If photographs don't exist, go to places he lived, if possible, and take pictures of buildings and streets or locate them in a travel magazine or online.

Gather everything you can find from your agency, and carefully record meetings with social workers, lawyers, and doctors that pertain to your child's history. Just as with younger children, and depending on what is in those documents, you may have to keep many of them separate from the life book until he's an adult and capable of emotionally and intellectually understanding his background.

Documenting Important Milestones for Preschool Kids

Your child may have lived in different places and under different circumstances. His life book will be essential for him to process who he was, who he is now, and who he will become. To create the life book for a preschooler:

- Find out where he was born and as much about his biological family as possible. If he was born in another country and abandoned to an orphanage, you might not have much direct information, but do your best.
- Include pictures, and other mementos of your travel to bring your child home in the book, even if you only drove to the other side of town.
- Include your first observations, statements from foster home or orphanage personnel, and others who interacted with you.
- Have your child draw pictures of his life before you, then write down his verbal explanation of what is depicted in the drawing.
- Ask him questions about his caregivers and write down what he remembers.
- Incorporate the material you sent to him before he came home with you.

Periodically, encourage your child to draw pictures about himself and his place in your family for his life book. Add your own observations to the pictures, and continue to photograph every important event and many ordinary ones. You and your child will enjoy watching the physical and emotional changes when you sit down together to read the pages.

Document What's Happening Now

Keep records, along with the scrapbooks and journals you fill out weekly or monthly. You may only have time to jot dates and brief comments and toss them into envelopes or boxes, but try to do something once or twice a month. Making your child's life concrete gives him tangible evidence that you love him and his life has meaning. Your efforts will forge attachments over the years.

CHAPTER 10

Adoption of Elementary School–Aged Children

Adopting an elementary school–aged child can be wonderful because he may be able to communicate well with you and do a lot of fun activities with your family without the intensive physical care babies or young children need. However, if your elementary-aged child comes from a deprived background or if he didn't receive adequate, loving care, he may be developmentally delayed, suffer from post-traumatic stress disorder, or have other emotional illnesses. In order to help him move forward, you will need to recreate the nurturing infancy and early childhood that are crucial for normal development and maturation.

Preparing Before the Placement

As with infants, toddlers, and preschoolers, you can do much to prepare for your elementary school child ahead of time. The training you received from your agency should have warned you about the high-structure and high-nurturing style of parenting demanded by adoption of older children. It will definitely not be a typical parenting experience.

You must help your child progress through the five levels of attachment that will allow her to begin formal education and move out into the world. Read about these levels so that you understand what to expect. She should:

- Trust and expect you to meet her needs (Level 1)
- Prefer you over anyone else and look to you for reassurance (Level 2)
- Seek your approval and feel guilty when you disapprove (Level 3)
- Want hugs and snuggles from you and imitate your behavior (Level 4)
- Be able to make friends and be eager to try to master new skills (Level 5)

Note that these levels of attachment are defined by child development specialists and apply to preschoolers as well.

Learn about Your Child's Background

When possible, it is important that you find out why your child became available for adoption, because you must know whether she was abandoned, removed from her biological parents because of their substance abuse or criminal conduct, or if the reason was more benign (as far as attachment goes), such as the illness or death of her parents. Understanding her history will help you understand what she is dealing with and reacting to.

Whatever the reason for your child's being placed for adoption and becoming part of your family, it may cause unique problems stemming from grief over the loss of her biological family and fear of the unknown (which is what you will initially represent).

Emotional Needs

Children between the ages of five to nine normally develop socially and intellectually at a significant pace. They learn to read, do math, study history and geography, and solve abstract problems. However, your child will likely lag behind her peers, because of disruptions in schooling and or upheavals at home.

Alert!

As with preschoolers, elementary school-aged children who have not been nourished properly may demonstrate cognitive delays and be underweight and/or shorter than normal. Sometimes, these deficiencies can be overcome with special diets and tutoring. Take your child to a pediatrician who specializes in physical and emotional challenges for children from deprived backgrounds or institutionalization.

Like any child, your child needs love, affection, and safety to develop well. For children of this age, friendships are also important. Your child may not have had the opportunity to develop friendships if she has been frequently moved from home to home. Children raised in orphanages may have formed deep attachments to the other children they were with, and separating from them and trying to make new friends who don't speak the same language or have the same background can be extremely difficult.

Physical Needs

Personal space is important for personality development in any growing child, but it doesn't have to be a whole room. Act on your knowledge of your child's background and be sure her room isn't totally isolated from the rest of the family. For example, don't remodel a basement playroom as a bedroom if the rest of the family's rooms are upstairs.

An ideal arrangement could be sharing a room that has a divider that can be closed once in awhile with a sibling of the same gender. "Once in awhile" is the operative phrase; you don't want her to spend extended time alone. Children who have attachment issues have been conditioned to only trust themselves, and the more time they're alone, the more powerfully that point is reinforced.

Set up her room in a welcoming way. Correspond with her and her caretakers to find out her interests, and incorporate those into the decor. For example, if you find out your adopted daughter loves horses, seeing a horse motif in her room may ease the awkwardness of transition.

 Essential

> If your child is having trouble making friends, help her understand the social cues or messages she's sending. Videotape her on the playground and watch the tape together. Help her see how her behavior signals to others whether she's friendly, afraid, or aggressive. It can take repeated conversations and a great amount of practice before your child can easily interact with peers in an age-appropriate manner.

Many adoptable children of elementary school age may never have owned much of anything; consequently, sharing will be a foreign concept. Understanding ownership must happen before your child will be comfortable enough to relinquish control enough for someone to play with one of her toys or even sit near her in a classroom.

Acting Out

Your child will spend his first few days with you on his best behavior, especially if you aren't his first placement. Therapists call this stage a "honeymoon," because it's artificial and doesn't represent real life. The older a child is, the longer the honeymoon can last. Deep down, your child will be terrified that you, too, will turn away and disappear, and he will struggle to do everything in his power to stop you from going. But, barring serious mental illness, he will soon become comfortable enough to start testing his boundaries.

Your child knows that he's weak and can't defend himself. He may never have been able to attach to a safe adult, so he's caught in the quandary of instinctively understanding his vulnerability but being unable to be comfortable with it.

His reaction to this problem may be to become withdrawn and go away emotionally to somewhere safe deep inside. He could appear catatonic; on the other hand, he could swagger around and pretend he's big and powerful. He may become preoccupied with violence, especially with guns and bombs and other mechanical devices that can make him feel he is strong and a force to be reckoned with.

As with toddlers and preschoolers, you must accept the responsibility to direct and control your child's acting out behavior, because he can't manage on his own. He probably hasn't progressed through the levels of attachment that would allow him to become autonomous and regulate himself in social and educational situations. It's up to you to show him what behavior is acceptable in your home and to help him mold his actions to the house rules.

Establish Developmentally Appropriate Boundaries

Until your child trusts you, you will have a difficult time figuring out and setting up boundaries. Also, unless you establish boundaries, attachment won't grow and trust won't develop—it's a paradox that you must solve!

Research indicates that you can take control of your child. Confer with your spouse or partner, decide what your behavior expectations are of your child, and then present a united front. You may also need input from your pediatrician or other adoption professional to be sure your expectations are reasonable. Because your child might be delayed in a number of ways, it is important to have expectations that correspond to your child's developmental age rather than his actual physical age.

Appropriate boundaries for elementary school–age children include:

- No hitting, yelling, or other hurtful actions
- Ask permission to leave the house
- Put dirty clothes in laundry baskets

- Sit at the table to eat dinner
- Regular bathing
- Attend school (once she is ready)
- Participate in the family by doing chores
- Participate in fun family activities in a way that is enjoyable for all family members

When you assign chores, keep things simple at first, then add chores like loading the dishwasher, cleaning the bathroom sink, and so on as your child can handle them.

Offer Immediate, Logical Consequences

You were probably told in your adoption training that you would need to be a highly structured parent. Elementary school–aged children who haven't been parented adequately may behave inappropriately. Many of them will have been exposed to adult situations and forced into adult roles they were neither physically nor mentally capable of shouldering. Therefore, they will have to unlearn certain behavior, such as kicking, slapping, or punching when they are angry or frustrated.

If your son hits a classmate who takes his place on the swings at recess, he's displaying the only behavior he's learned. You have to help him find and use a better method. Acknowledge his feelings of frustration: "You really wanted to swing and were upset that Devin got there first."

Then point out that hitting Devin hurts him and that your child got into trouble with the playground aide because of this. Describe the consequences of hurting someone at school: "You can't play at recess for a whole week," and ask your child what he could have done instead of hitting. Don't accept a shrug or "I dunno." Gently say, "You could have stamped your foot and said, 'I'm mad that you have the swing.' It's okay to be upset, but it's not okay to hit."

It can be helpful to help your child act out difficult situations like this so that you can arm him with appropriate responses and behaviors. Don't expect one talk to make everything clear for him though. He has years of learned behaviors to unlearn and this can take time.

Calming Fears

If your elementary child has come from a neglectful situation, her most common fears are that she won't have enough to eat or adequate clothing and shelter, and being hurt or abandoned. She probably experienced either a sterile environment, as in an orphanage, or a chaotic environment, if she was removed from her biological family.

Hoarding food, being unable to sleep, restlessness, and resisting hugs or displays of affection are all indicators that your child doesn't feel safe, even though she's in your home. Her mind may know that she's in a far different place, but her body and nervous system are in a state of panic. Only time, coupled with loving connections, will relieve her panic.

Fear of Hunger

As with preschoolers, you may find your child sneaking food out of the kitchen and stashing it under her bed, in her closet, or other easily accessible places. She may slip food from the table into her pockets or wrap it in a napkin and stow it under her shirt during meal times. Watch for this kind of behavior and reassure your child that she can eat all she wants during the meal, but that food can spoil and make her sick if it isn't in the refrigerator. Discuss with her what kinds of snacks she'd like to keep in her room or in a place in the cupboards that is hers to go to whenever she feels hungry.

Alert!

Another way to calm hunger fears is to feed each other. Cut up an apple (or other enjoyable, pleasant food) and pop pieces of it into his mouth. Then let him feed you. This reciprocity activates calming hormones from the primitive areas of his brain that have to do with survival.

Give your child some control over how and when food is served. You might let her suggest some foods or meals. Let her help you prepare it and put it into serving bowls. Teach her how to set the table and make dinner time a special family time. Partaking of food together is a bonding activity and one that should be indulged in on a regular basis.

Fear That Keeps Her Awake

You may find that your child is unable to relax enough to fall asleep. She may be in a state of hypervigilance, a state that helped her survive on the streets or in a home that was dangerous. When your child first comes home to you, you should know something about where she slept and under what circumstances.

Help your child understand that she's safe in a clean bed, with you nearby. At first, you may have to make a bed on the floor of your room, so you can be there if she wakes up with nightmares.

At bedtime, figure out calming activities that will signal it's safe to quiet down and prepare for sleep. Develop a nighttime ritual that includes a snack, a story and or song, and quiet talk about pleasant things, especially good experiences.

Fear of Trust

Your child may have been the victim of physical abuse and, therefore, have little or no frame of reference for the affectionate exchanges that occurs in most functional families. You can be sure that this is the case if your child recoils if you make a sudden move toward her or if she never meets your gaze.

Be very careful about making sudden moves, and if you do so and she startles, apologize and step back. But don't make the mistake of avoiding physical contact because it makes her nervous. There are many ways to begin the "dance of affection" without stirring up horrible emotions in your child.

Start by keeping her close by, in the same room. Take opportunities to sit beside her, reading to her or talking about the weather, a family pet, or other neutral topic. After a while, she may lean against you or indicate in other ways that she's comfortable with the level of contact.

Once your child becomes comfortable being next to you, begin to make affectionate overtures, such as lightly touching her hair, shoulder, or hand and progressing to a gentle pat. Point out that moms and dads and other members of a family hug each other. School-aged children can understand the differences, intellectually, between good touch and bad touch. You may need a therapist to help you get beyond the hair- or shoulder-patting stage if serious abuse has occurred.

 Essential

Family interactions, such as board games, conversation, and old-fashioned parlor games like charades, build brain and emotional attachments. Set aside at least one day a week for a family night; take the phone off the hook and focus on having fun together.

Not looking into your eyes is a way for your child to disconnect from you and to retreat into herself. It's sort of like that old caricature of an ostrich with its head in the sand; if your child can't see you, she's thinks she's not vulnerable.

From the beginning of your relationship, you can say gently, "Sweetie, look at me" or "I want to see your pretty brown eyes" or other methods of initiating eye contact. You can also say, "When you look at me, I know you hear me" or "I'm much more interesting than the floor."

As you would with any child, help her identify who is safe and who isn't. Say things like:

- Safe people treat you with kindness.
- Safe people never ask you to keep secrets from your parents.

- Safe people don't touch you where your bathing suit would cover.
- Safe people don't do things that make you uncomfortable.

If you are dealing with serious issues, ask your child's therapist for help.

Adoption experts experienced in attachment problems recommend that you pursue a child who tries to avoid you physically or emotionally. Obviously, your pursuit cannot seem threatening or intrusive. Some parents have found that simple things like setting the child's place at the table close to them or keeping up a conversation when they leave the room helps calm children who are afraid of adults.

Meeting Your Elementary-Aged Child's Unique Challenges

You already know that a child who has suffered multiple placements, neglect, and or abuse may act out with violent behaviors or withdraw into himself. He will probably have health, emotional, and mental issues. If your child is in this situation, the best thing you can do is to maintain consistent, nonthreatening physical closeness, eye contact, calm communication, and encouragement of reciprocating kindnesses. If you are stymied by how to figure out responses that will calm or draw out your child, ask your pediatrician, therapist, or member of your support group for suggestions.

Physical Health Issues

Your child may have come to you undernourished or in a physically poor state. If he wasn't fed adequately or given the opportunity for exercise, his body and brain have not developed properly. You can draw on many experts to help you understand and heal your child's body and brain. See the appendices for specific tips and resources.

Keep in mind that besides eating a proper balance of foods, your child needs to exercise to properly assimilate nutrients. Oxygen and glucose get to his brain through his bloodstream, a process that becomes more efficient with exercise.

Fact

Not only do video games, television, and personal electronics take time away from brain-building exercise, but these diversions are antisocial and can get in the way of building attachments. Either eliminate or severely restrict them when you are working on building attachment.

You must get your child moving; exercise tones muscles, especially the brain. Take walks and ride bicycles together, sign up for a sport together, or offer to coach a youth league that your child participates in. If the weather is stormy, play catch inside with a spongy ball or put on an exercise video or jazzy CD and dance around the room together.

Cultural Issues

If you adopt an older child from a different culture, your challenges will be compounded by language and societal barriers. You'll spend huge amounts of time helping that child adjust. For example, if you adopt a child like May Lin, a Vietnamese six-year-old orphan, you'll have a child who knows only three English words, "hi," "yes," and "no." As you teach her your language, she'll teach you some of hers.

As her adoptive parent, you'll encourage May Lin to reminisce about the place she left behind. You will help her deal with the grief of losing everything she's ever known, even if what she knew was privation and neglect. See Chapters 5 and 6 for more ideas about dealing with children from other countries or outside your ethnic group.

Dealing with the Past

Your elementary-aged child knows, mentally, emotionally, and physically, that he had a family before coming to you. If he knew his birth parents, that family may have been completely dysfunctional, even dangerous, but it is still a part of him. He may feel grief over losing everything familiar, rage at the treatment he received, or guilt about being removed from the home. If your child never knew his birth parents or lived in a home, he will still grieve for them even though he does not remember them. You should help him through his grief by acknowledging it and affirming his right to grieve, as well as his right to be angry, because adults who should have loved and cared for him were unable to do so.

Tell your child that he was in no way responsible for the break up of his home or the inability of his parents to care for him. He did nothing wrong and he wasn't a bad child. He may want to believe you, but his stored memories will confuse the issue. If you realize that your child isn't processing his emotions well, take him to a therapist. Most therapists recommend that counseling involve the whole core family, because of the attachment issues involved.

Help Others Understand Your Child's Behavior

When friends note that you've added to your family, they will be curious and want to know about your experience. Your family, of course, will want to know details and consider how they fit into the picture. Others, like teachers, coaches, and car-pool parents, will need some information. Your challenge will be to assess who has a need to know (and to what degree) and who is merely being snoopy. Respect your child's right to privacy and to control her own story.

Your child may be withdrawn, make little eye contact, and seem excessively shy. On the other hand, she may swagger around, tell outrageous stories, or be belligerent. She may start fights, use foul language, or have other unacceptable behaviors. These behaviors can be confusing, even frightening, to others.

Question?

How do I answer questions about why my child never looks anyone in the eyes and flinches when somebody approaches her?
You can simply say that she has been in situations where it wasn't safe to trust anybody and that you are working with her on the issue. If the person asking is a family member who is also part of your support group, you may need to share more specifics. But remember that her history is hers; be sensitive about sharing details with those who have a need to know.

If you have been well prepared for her placement, you will have been taught strategies to control negative behavior. Be sure you've taken the time you need to integrate your child into the family, at least long enough (and with the help of a therapist, if necessary) for her to accept that she's home and that you are the parent. Until this acceptance occurs, your child will not be able to function well away from you.

Dealing with School Issues

Learning to relate to others is an essential life skill. Elementary-aged children must learn social skills such as sharing and empathy. In our culture, social skills are first formed in the home, then in the school system.

If your child has endured privations and abuse, he will probably be developmentally behind his peers and will need special attention and help to catch up. If your child has come to you from another country, he will most certainly need help as he struggles to learn your language, culture, and environment. It's your job to be sure he gets that attention and help at school. Your placement agency should provide advice and post-adoption support—especially pertaining to what kind of education he should have and finding therapists and counselors.

Public School

With the guidance of your support group, assess your child's unique situation. Consider his language skills, his ability to understand cause and effect, and most importantly, his trust in and attachment to you. He will accept your decision to give him into the care of teachers when he's ready. Public school programs vary by state, and yours may have an intervention program for children with speech and cognitive delays. There may also be a special program for nonnative English speakers, also called English as a Second Language (ESL).

You will have to decide which educational route is best for your child. If he comes to you from a foreign orphanage, the language barrier can make him very uncomfortable in a public school setting, but he'll learn English more readily if he's around other children. Also, unless you speak his language fluently, you won't be able to teach him much at home. With input from your trusted support system and adoption professionals, you can figure out just how to get his education started and focused.

Other Educational Options

You may have to try a private school or homeschooling, as well as traditional public school, before you find the right fit. If private schools are too expensive, do what many parents do—join a homeschooling association, like the American Homeschool Association, and band together with other parents to combine the best qualities of private and homeschools. Only you and your child's therapist can determine exactly what educational path to follow. You will also need to meet your state's homeschooling laws if you choose to educate him at home.

If you have a homeschooling group, your child can get personal attention, while combining field trips, sporting events, and specialized classes like music and art in the company of other homeschooled children. This arrangement will give him the socialization he needs, while keeping him close to you until he's ready for the wider world.

Recordkeeping

Your elementary-aged child probably had many experiences before she joined your family. But, her life is her reality, and there's nothing you can do to erase the past. Helping her move out of that past into her present with you will be your primary job. By doing so, you connect with her where she is and validate yourself as a parent she will be able to trust implicitly. Making the abstractions of her life more concrete through pictures and words will give both of you the tools to examine that life and to enhance the joy and deal with the pain.

Find Out What Happened in the Past

Start with your social worker or whoever placed your child in your home. If your child came from foster care, ask for contact information for members of her extended biological family, especially if there are restraining orders against her biological parents. If you are not your child's first out-of-family placement, contact those who cared for her previously. Try to get pictures of people and places who were part of her past.

Find out where she was born and take a picture of the hospital, if possible. Cut out pictures from old magazines that illustrate what was going on in her world when she was a particular age. Encourage people who knew her as a baby, toddler, and or preschooler to tell you about her.

If your child came from another country, assemble photos you took while there and all the information you gathered when you were completing the adoption.

Find out if your child has siblings or was close to other children in the orphanage or foster home. Get pictures of those children, or ask workers to describe them and the activities they shared.

Some of the information you collect may not be appropriate for your child to know now, so put court documents, arrest warrants, and such in a separate place. You can give such information to your child when she's an adult and capable of processing that part of her life. For now, keep, but don't share, it.

Document Life as It Is Now

Your older adopted child could come to you with many unresolved difficulties and feelings. You may feel overwhelmed with sorrow at times, as well as have great anger toward those who neglected her. Don't let your feelings weigh you down or stop you from realizing that a far better life story is being written for her.

The more concrete you can make her story and the more you can include her in the creation of it, the stronger your bond with her will become. One excellent way to have her participate is to give her a journal in which both of you will write about the events of the day (or week, depending on the time you can commit). Many parents use bedtime to write in the journal. You may find, as she grows more comfortable with you, that she will tell you things about her previous life. Writing those things down and discussing them can be very cathartic and healing.

Take pictures of your child inside your house, beside you and your spouse, and with other children in the family. Also, take pictures of your neighborhood, with her riding her bike or zipping along on in-line skates or cartwheeling on the lawn. Commemorate as many important moments as you can: first day in a new grade, activities with friends, sporting events. Preparing and maintaining this life book will let your child see just how much you love her, and that she really is a part of your family.

CHAPTER 11

Adoption of
Tweens and Teens

Adolescence (between the ages of twelve and twenty) is a time of turmoil, change, and surging toward adulthood for all children, but it's especially challenging for adopted adolescents. You are adopting a child who will, unlike an infant or a small child, only depend on you for a relatively few number of years. But in those years, you can make a profound difference in her life.

Preparing for the Placement

Adopting an adolescent means that your serious struggles are far shorter than the twenty-plus years you must devote to an infant. Of course, you also miss out on the cute stages that nature provided to cushion against what many people think of as a terrible time of life.

Find out all you can about the adolescent period of growth, because current research has revealed some fascinating information about how your child's brain develops at this age, and the fact that many behaviors exhibited at this age are biologically driven.

Learn about Adolescent Behaviors

Like most people, you probably never gazed into your spouse or partner's eyes and said, "Let's have a teenager" instead of "Let's have a baby." Adoptive teens are given a bad rap, though. In the opinion of most experts, given good parenting, even if it's long delayed, most teens turn into reasonably good and happy people. Human children are remarkably resilient; those who spend eleven, thirteen, or sixteen years bouncing back and forth between dysfunctional families and foster homes can make great progress when they finally attain parents who love and want them. In reality, adopting a teen involves much less physical and emotional effort than adopting younger children. Teens also have the cognitive ability to understand the difference between good and bad families.

 Fact

You should know that adolescent brains have only a slight capacity for logical thought. Studies like those published in *The Secret Life of The Brain* by Richard Restak reveal that when brains reach adult size, the synapses in the frontal lobe (where organizational, logical thoughts are processed) begin to connect. Scans of adolescent brains in action show the emotional centers as very active, with very little activity in the frontal lobe.

More and more frequently, public and private agencies are urging the adoption of children over ten, especially teens who will age out of the system when they turn eighteen. Behavioral scientists and therapists such as Dr. David Walsh, therapist and research expert into adolescent brain function and author of *Why Do They Act That Way?* know what most parents have always known—eighteen year olds are rarely ready to assume all responsibility for their lives. The rewiring of adolescent brains that starts at about age ten continues well into the mid-twenties, and sometimes, especially with boys, isn't finished until the early thirties.

Understand Your Child's Situation

You should know that, in many ways, your teen has much in common with a toddler. She lives in the moment and operates almost completely on emotion. In addition, her brain is awash in the hormones that are turning her into an adult.

Plus, your child is much bigger than a toddler and cannot be restrained physically very easily. Your challenge will be to provide the nurturing and boundaries your teen requires to allow her brain to reconnect and to finish changing into an adult.

In addition to the normal changes and stresses of adolescence, your adopted teen's struggles may be more intense, because of her dual identities: she's been defined by her birth family and is now transitioning into yours.

 **Alert!**

Teens always challenge their parents to varying degrees; such behavior is psychologically necessary for establishing an independent adult identity and is not caused by adoption. Be aware that adoption may be one of the reasons your teen uses to explain his frustrations and disagreements with you, or his feelings of alienation and loneliness. As in any developmental stage, adoption can be a layer of the problem that a teen is facing.

An adopted teen may in fact be easier to deal with than other teens. Organizations such as the Adoption Institute, the Ad Council in partnership with the U.S. Department of Health and Human Services, and AdoptUsKids have initiated a campaign encouraging adoption of teens. They assert that adopted children in their mid-teens are less likely to indulge in rejecting behavior than biological children or children adopted as infants. Your daughter will know, unless she has severe psychological problems, the importance of a stable family and will probably give you far less trouble than the teen children of your friends!

Celebrating Your Child's Homecoming

Adding a new member to your family is cause for celebration. Just how you celebrate will be defined by several factors:

- Age
- Personality
- How long she's waited for a family
- Your family's culture

If your child is eleven or twelve (give or take a year or two), consider throwing a family party, complete with decorated cake, party favors, and presents. Hang a banner with the words "Welcome to the Jones Family" and place it over the front door or in the yard, if appropriate.

 Essential

Because your teen will feel unsure at first, mark the first month, six months, and then every year thereafter with a celebration. Develop a tradition around the "Placement Day." Sing to her, hide presents around the room, put a notice in the local newspaper, or let her pick all the foods for dinner. Repeating these activities in the same way, over time, will do much to forge family ties.

Your older teen may want something more adult and restrained—perhaps keeping the banner indoors—but she'll still like gifts! Consider your family's culture; if you generally make a fuss over birthdays, graduations, and holidays, do the same for celebrating the arrival of a teen. Having fun together is a basic bonding activity for all families and is especially important in adoption.

For example, when Amy was adopted at age twelve, her parents held a placement celebration with their friends and family and important people to Amy, including her counselor, social worker, guardian ad litem, and foster family. Her new dad promised to be a loving father and to protect and provide for her. Her new mom also made similar promises and gave Amy gifts that represented those promises: a quilt, a charm bracelet with charms that represented certain things from her past, and an original poem.

Knowing When the Honeymoon Is Over

Teens or tweens who have endured multiple disruptions and emotional or physical abuse can be desperate for a "real" family. Your teen may never have known a mom's tender touch or the companionship and example of a competent, caring dad. He probably blames himself for the failings of his biological parents and thinks, deep down, that if he had tried harder, he wouldn't have lost his family. So, he will do everything in his power to please you when he first joins your family. This period, the honeymoon, is the same for adopted toddlers, school-aged children, and tweens and teens.

Alert!

As your child becomes more assured, she will gradually become comfortable enough to test your commitment. You can partially avoid some of the worst testing if you acknowledge the "I don't care" and overly compliant behavior as what it is—fear of rejection. Be sure that you do the acknowledgment in private, and not in front of other people.

Your I-don't-care adolescent is shut down emotionally. He's been hurt and disappointed so many times he's retreated into himself and won't risk loving you. Your overly compliant child is trying to earn his way into your heart. He's terrified he'll mess up and be rejected, so he's willing to become the family slave to avoid being hurt again. He is also shut down, but in a different way.

From the moment you decide to adopt, you must let your teen know that he's not on trial, that you and the rest of the family have declared him part of your inner circle, and the contract is for keeps. Reassurance comes in many different, often subtle, ways: gentle touch, kind words, and clear expectations that will reinforce your position as the adult in charge. Your teen has probably been forced to rely totally on himself, and has a deeply ingrained mistrust for authority and adults. He needs to know you won't give up on him, that your love isn't conditional, and that he can relax and be parented.

Unique Challenges for Adolescents

According to statistics kept by the U.S. Department of Health and Welfare, your teen or tween child probably became available for adoption because her biological family failed her. Nearly 80 percent of adoptable teens from foster care have parents with addiction and or criminal problems. The rest have parents with serious mental or physical illnesses or who have died.

Recognize that your tween or teen has needs similar to a much younger child's—the innate desire to be nurtured and kept safe. These things didn't happen for her; she grew up quickly, forced to do so by the need to survive, so her childhood needs were ignored or blocked, yet they remain part of her psyche.

Overcoming Emotional Deficiencies

Accept your child's past. While acknowledging that her birth mom or dad should have done better, you can say, "Look at what an amazing person you are because of your life experiences." Do not be surprised if your teen rebukes you. An adolescent who has lived years in an abusive and or neglectful home generally has damaged self-esteem. Until she feels better about herself, she may cynically reject compliments.

Letting go of anger and feelings of betrayal happens when you and your child are able to forgive. Forgiveness doesn't mean accepting bad behavior or enabling continued abuse; but forgiveness does calm a racing heart and churning stomach. It's a physical as well as emotional and spiritual phenomenon that results in great peace.

Overcoming Social Deficiencies

You can do a lot to help your child fit into her peer group. She may not have good social skills or may be unable to read the body language of others. You may need to point out that talking about bodily functions is inappropriate in a group setting, or need to tell her that a harsh tone of voice offends, even if the words seem okay.

 Essential

Remember, children, especially adolescents, aren't mind readers. They need clear, concrete guidelines and reinforcement. Like all human beings, they'll repeat the behavior that meets their needs. Don't assume your child knows you appreciate him taking out the garbage without being asked—tell him!

Talk about what was offensive or rude, and what your child can do or say differently next time. Develop a signal that you can use in public to let your teen know she needs to rephrase something or apologize. For example, if she's making a nuisance of herself by grabbing a friend or taking over a conversation, you can use a code word or phrase like, "Did you unplug the iron before we left?" to let her know she should back off.

Conversely, catch your teen doing well and point it out. When your teen deftly handles a social situation or avoids saying something she shouldn't, praise her. Discuss (again in private) how pleased you are with her progress.

Bond with Your Adolescent

Your new addition to the family needs connection and attention initially just as much as a much younger child. Keep in mind that this adult-looking person is really a vulnerable child inside, a child who has built up layers and layers of defenses and coping methods.

Finding one-on-one time will be your most effective way to start the attachment process. During your teen's first year with you, you or your partner may want to take a leave of absence from work or to postpone business trips that involve long absences from home, so that you can spend more time with him. At the very least, it is a good idea to try to rearrange your schedule so that an adult is home when he gets home from school each day.

Establish Family Rituals

All cultures and all families develop rituals. Think about how you can bring those rituals into play to help foster ties to your new child. Family dinners at least once a week, especially when you include extended family, are great bonding opportunities.

Try grocery shopping together with your child or wandering the aisles of a gift shop on Friday afternoons after school. Play cards, go out to dinner, and sit in the bleachers to cheer for your teen's school at football or soccer games.

 *Question?*

How can I find alone time with my child?
Families today spend a lot of time traveling to various destinations. Use the time to visit or listen to the radio or CD player together. Don't let your teen bring iPods or other personal electronics, including cell phones (and turn yours off), because these items encourage withdrawal and disconnection.

If your teen likes sports, music, drama, or art, check out the resources in your town. Your first stop could be the library or department of parks and recreation. These institutions welcome volunteers and usually have all sorts of activities like story hours, book reading, or writing contests, craft classes, and oil painting lessons.

Find ways to develop interests that you can share, like trying out for a community play. If neither of you wins a part, volunteer to sew costumes or paint scenery together. Join a service group, offer to coach a team, help the drama teacher build sets, or chaperone a field trip. The emphasis with your teen needs to be regular, positive involvement that builds mutual trust and understanding.

Help Your Child Accept Appropriate Touch

Your teen who was physically or sexually abused or who witnessed such abuse may be unable to distinguish between hurtful, inappropriate touching and the physical connections that build attachments between family members. This kind of problem almost always needs long-term therapy, but you can do a lot to help him understand that it is healthy for family members to look into each other's eyes and give and receive hugs.

 **Alert!**

> Always start out with light pats on the shoulder or hair and progress to one-armed hugs. Help your child understand that touching builds attachment, but don't force the issue. You should re-enforce that he look into your eyes when you talk by patiently waiting until he looks at you before you continue talking in a conversation with him.

A mom described how her older children helped Janet when she was first adopted at age thirteen. "She was really strained with the boys, who were eighteen, twenty, and twenty-one at the time. They were all very good about not hugging her, giving her space to get used to them, and teasing in a playful but safe manner. Eventually, she warmed up to all of them."

Help Your Adolescent Prepare for Independence

Some tweens or teens are too mature for their ages because their life circumstances didn't allow them to be children. Nobody took care of them, and instead, they cared for themselves, and often, younger siblings as well. Frequently, this can be seen in adopted teens who attempt to take parental roles with younger siblings in the family or try to be sexual with older siblings. Other teens learned to survive by being compliant and dependent to the point where they will actively compete with much young children in the family for your time and undivided attention.

Assess where your child is on the continuum toward maturity. Then plan, with your family therapist or support group if necessary, how to slow down a child who is prematurely adult or how to assist one who is delayed.

Provide Structure and Continuity

Your teen probably lives in the moment, not only because of her disconnecting brain, but because the past was painful and the future is vague. Help her understand self-advocacy and how to take responsibility for actions. Self-advocacy involves setting and working toward life goals. It means shrugging off a victim attitude and taking self-control in the form of self-discipline and self-confidence, rather than oppositional power struggles.

Writing things down will help you and your teen think about abstract concepts in concrete terms. Charts and lists are practical ways to focus attention and teach skills. For example, if your daughter has poor hygiene, you can make up a list that contains personal grooming activities such as "brush teeth," "wash hands before eating," and "bathe before bed" that she checks off each day. Don't just post the list and forget about it; talk about it, and come up with motivators that will prompt her to follow through.

 Essential

Being able to play computer games, listen to music, watch TV or videos, and spend time with friends are all examples of motivators for most teens. Let your child help you figure out the specifics, because rewarding only works if the reward is something he wants.

Make up a chart that tracks whether or not the lists were followed and the rewards that were earned. Your adolescent will need frequent talks and interaction, especially as you set schedules and award the motivators. However, don't start using the lists and charts unless you're committed to following through with them.

If just thinking about such big organizational projects gives you a headache, you may want to stick with making notes on a piece of paper so you can remember what you and your teen agreed upon and go over the notes at regular intervals during one-on-one times.

Face Educational Issues

Sporadic school attendance may have been a part of your child's previous life, and you will be challenged to help her make up missed work. Like most adoptive parents, you will probably spend countless hours meeting with teachers and administrators before your adolescent finally settles into school.

Remember that you are your child's advocate, and nobody cares about her as much as you do. The law says that your school district must provide an appropriate education, adapted to your child's special needs, but you will be hard pressed to be sure she gets it.

You may decide to homeschool your teen or tween her first year with you, while enrolling her in sports, scouts, and other outside activities for socialization. Or you may place her in a private school, where you will volunteer frequently.

 **Fact**

> The Coleman-Landrieu amendment to the Higher Education Access Act expands the definition of "independent student" to allow a student's financial aid eligibility to be determined solely by the student's ability to pay, regardless of the adoptive family's income level. This will make college accessible to many adopted children.

Life Lessons

Depending on your child's age and previous experiences, you will want to provide age-appropriate lessons. Children under fourteen or fifteen shouldn't have to worry about whether or not there's enough money to pay the electric bill or make the mortgage payment. Your teen needs permission to be a young person, to avoid worrying about family finances and whether there will be food on the table.

On the other hand, your teen should be aware that the family has finite funds. Even if you can afford to buy your teen $250 name-brand athletic shoes, think twice about indulging such materialism. Help her distinguish between wants and needs; reassure her that her needs will always be met in her new family, but that everybody must learn to delay gratification. The difference between wants and needs varies with individual families; your specific values will dictate the difference.

Learning to play a musical instrument has been shown to help children's brains reconnect and build neurons that have been damaged through abuse and neglect. So, do encourage your teen to try an instrument, but rent one. Don't buy it until real interest and follow through has been demonstrated. Most schools have loan or rental programs.

Alert!

Be sure that your teen completes any courses, lessons, or team sign-ups. Don't allow her to drop out once the commitment has been made. Sticking with something that turns out to be harder than expected builds character. The exception to this is when a situation triggers your teen's anxiety and traumatic responses due to past experiences. Use empathic listening and understanding to determine if an activity is too overwhelming.

Deal with Peer Pressures

All teens shift their focus to the wider world outside their families as they progress toward adulthood. This shift is normal, but your new adolescent likely didn't have a normal childhood, so he probably attached to his peers in an abnormal way, or was rejected by them and has social problems.

Dealing with peer pressures (real or perceived) is difficult emotionally and intellectually. Remind your teen and yourself that your job as her parent is to teach him appropriate behavior to help him fit into and attach to your family. Part of this is helping him learn to cope with the problems thrown his way by his peer group.

Get a Handle on Inappropriate Behavior

You may find that, before entering your family, your teen ran around all night because nobody cared where he was or what he did. He may have had a girlfriend and experimented with sex or been exposed to it at a tender age. Curfews and dating are very real and serious issues, because they relate directly to your family's values.

If your fifteen-year-old teen has already been sexually active and such activity is against your values, you will need support from social services and therapists. If you are unsure how to handle this issue, don't follow through with the adoption until you are clear in your own mind about what you expect and how you are going to provide supervision, information about protection against STDs, and birth control. See Chapter 17 for more information.

Recordkeeping

Assembling the story of your child's life can be one of your greatest gifts to her. Your efforts to contact her biological family and find out that she had a puppy when she was six or that she played Little League in the third grade and her team won the sportsmanship trophy will be valuable to your child.

You may have a hard time finding anything if your child was placed in protective custody by the state, and you may have acquired a lot of negative information about your child's circumstances in the course of your adoption. Keep those kinds of records separate from more benign information.

Finding Elusive Records

The agency who placed your child should have records that you can read and copy. Court documents should also be available to you. Current privacy laws may make access difficult, but do your best.

You shouldn't sugar coat the negative things that happened in your child's life. Your child may very well have a truant record at school or have been in trouble with the law. However, separate the negative material about her or her biological family and put it in a private place if it's anything that can be extremely uncomfortable to remember. Your teen will eventually be able to deal with the realities of her painful past, but that might not happen until she's much older.

Assemble historical information from newspapers for your child's birth date, the day she entered kindergarten, and other important dates. Find out where she lived and what was going on at the time. Sports and entertainment events, including popular music, videos, and games, will add interest and fill in gaps.

Focus on the Present and the Positive

You and your child may wish with all your heart that you could have interceded and gathered her into your arms and protected her from the pain and neglect she faced in the past. Decide now that you will control the present by building a record for the rest of your child's life. You can spend oodles of money on special papers, forms, or ribbons for scrapbooking, but don't think you need to do so. Scrapbooking can be a bonding activity with your child, but you can have just as much fun with photographs and three-hole punched construction paper.

In addition to the material you gather from your teen's previous life to preserve in books and shadow boxes, assemble all paper work, newspaper clippings of current events, school papers and reports, and court documents from what's happening now into files to maintain until she's grown.

Develop a camera habit and snap pictures or videos of every important event, such as baseball games, band recitals, and birthdays. If you don't have time to paste things into scrapbooks, just keep them in dated envelopes and or folders.

Instead of looking back and being stuck in the ugliness and sorrow there, turn your attention to now, to repeatedly saying, "I love you, my child" and "This is your forever family."

CHAPTER 12

Adoption of Special Needs Children

This chapter addresses concerns you'll face if you adopt children with physical and or emotional disabilities such as blindness, cerebral palsy, fetal alcohol syndrome, Down syndrome, reactive attachment disorder (RAD), autism, and other disorders. See these children as human beings first, and deal with their disabilities second. Your child is much more like any other child than he is different; he has the same needs for nurturing, boundaries, and unconditional love as any other child.

Accept the Realities of Special Needs Children

By agreeing to adopt a child with serious physical and or emotional disabilities, you are doing something many people think is heroic or beyond the average person's capabilities. You, of course, know that love for a child and a willingness to give that child whatever is necessary drives your actions. Perhaps you do love more deeply than the ordinary parent, but your rewards also transcend anything anyone, except those who walk the same path, can imagine.

With the love and dedication you feel, you also know that you need to deal with your personal issues before taking on a special needs child. In addition, you must have access to respite care so you can recharge your emotional batteries on a regular basis.

Confront Your Grief

When you adopt a blind, deaf, or emotionally disturbed child, you must put aside fantasies about your son becoming a star athlete, member of the Blue Angels, or a Broadway headliner. Letting go of these fantasies is a kind of loss for you as a parent, and you must take the time to grieve for the future your child will never have.

In the abstract, before your child comes into your home, you may think it won't be so bad, but when you're faced with a frightened, angry five year old who wears diapers and can't speak in sentences, you will be stunned.

Your greatest strength will come from putting aside your preconceived notions and accepting your child on his terms, according to his reality. He may have a feeding tube and be unable to breathe on his own. Or he may go into rages and tear up toys and clothes and punch holes in the wall. Whatever the reality, you can handle it if you let go of your preconceived notions, recognize your need to heal, and have training and professional support, as well as a loving circle of friends and family.

Your Child's Grief

Experts have begun to realize how important dealing with grief can be, especially for special needs children. You know that this particular child is different from others his age. Because of his mental or physical problems, he may have been rejected by his biological family, or his biological parents may have relinquished him out of love and a desire for him to receive medical services they couldn't manage. However, no matter what the reason, he will feel rejected and needs to be able to work through his grief and anger at what has happened to him.

All adopted children wonder why those who gave birth to them didn't stick around to be parents, and they fear they were inadequate in some way. But a child with mental retardation, Fetal Alcohol Syndrome, autism, attention deficit hyperactivity disorder (ADHD), or other disability knows he doesn't walk, learn, or behave like other children and can think he's somehow broken. He will probably have erected emotional barriers and engaged in troubling behaviors; it's safer to throw a tantrum or lash out than to admit he doesn't understand. He needs to find a way to work through the emotions this causes.

Alert!

You may have a problem with your adoption process if you aren't given opportunities to interact with your child before placement, her foster parents are hostile or uncooperative, you have few details about her background, or are not allowed to see her medical records. Don't be deflected from your search to understand her better by references to privacy. You will be her parents and must have all pertinent information.

You will have to enter his reality and coax him into yours. Patience, persistence, and working with those who have studied his particular disorder will bring results.

Help Your Other Children Understand

A special needs child in the family can bring everybody together, promoting cooperation and unselfishness beyond the reach of those who have never faced similar challenges. But don't lose sight of the importance for everybody's needs to be met. Help your other children express themselves if they feel neglected because of the large amount of time you have to spend with your handicapped child.

Help your other children understand your new child's particular handicap. Many adoptive parents role-play with their children before the special needs sibling comes home. For example, if your future son suffers from low or no vision, have a family activity where members of the family wear blindfolds and try to do something like walk from one side of the room to another or make a bed. This effort will help develop sensitivity to what the new member faces all the time. Try similar activities for hearing loss by using ear plugs and trying to carry on a conversation.

Alert!

Some siblings may try to overcompensate by becoming too involved in the care of their handicapped sibling. When the child first comes into your home, there may be a sense of novelty, but quickly moving to normal family life will be best for everyone. You are the parent and should reassure your children that they don't have to be adults, that you will take responsibility. But thank them for their help.

Your children may be more understanding of physical handicaps than they are of mental or emotional dysfunctions. Learn together about the particular disability and how you can help the new child fit into the family.

Respite Care

All parents need backup, and parents of special needs children are no different. Respite care refers to a plan for care so that you can take a break from parenting. One option is to rely on family and friends to step in and provide child care. Another option is to work out a plan with your agency for respite foster care. Under this plan, your child will stay with trained and experienced foster parents who know how to work with disabilities. You can use respite care to take a vacation or just have some time to yourself.

Don't assume you can do everything on your own. Every parent needs a break, and it is best to think about how you will arrange respite care before you complete your adoption.

Prepare for the Placement

Just how you prepare will depend on the particular special need (or combination of needs) and age of your child. If your two-year-old daughter has sleep apnea and spinal bifida, you will need portable oxygen and a sturdy stroller. You'll also need the services of physical and occupational therapists who will help her achieve mobility. Your teenager with Down syndrome will need special education classes and a way to interact with her peers. Meeting physical and mental needs will be expensive, so it is important to understand exactly what needs there are and how they must be met before you adopt.

Find the Financial Resources You Need

Legislatures are finally beginning to recognize that special needs foster kids are difficult to place, mainly because of the excessively high cost of ongoing medical and psychiatric care and equipment. However, if you don't ask for financial help, nobody's going to offer it. It's a classic case of "the squeaky wheel gets the grease."

Financial resources are available to you, especially if you adopt your child from the foster care system, and your social worker should tell you how to apply. You may find that your child qualifies for social security and welfare payments through your state because of her situation before placement. You may also qualify for Adoption and Safe Families Act funding. This is a relatively new federal program that is administered differently by each state. If your child is legally disabled, she will also qualify for Medicaid.

 **Fact**

If your household income is under $150,000 per year, you are entitled to a $10,390 adoption tax credit, without proving expenses for your child (unlike with other adoptions, where you can only deduct your actual expenses). Depending on your circumstances, you may want to space it out over a few years. See your tax consultant for specifics about applying.

Keeping a child in foster care is much more expensive for the government than subsidizing an adoption. In addition, adopted children are much more emotionally healthy and their ultimate outcomes are many times better than those who stay in the system. Because of this, most states will enter into an Adoption Assistance Agreement, which lays out the state funding your child will receive after the adoption. Again, don't expect anyone to tell you about it unless you ask directly. Contact *www.nacac.org/subsidy_stateprofiles.html* for detailed information about programs available in your area.

Negotiate an adoption assistance agreement with your state, regardless of whether you adopt through a private or public agency or whether you enter into a kinship adoption. Don't finalize the special needs adoption until your agreement is in place. It should:

- Be in writing
- State amounts and duration of the payments
- Specify reporting requirements
- Indicate any agreements made about respite care

Get legal advice before you sign. The stakes are too high for you to rely on your emotions alone.

Setting Up Your House

In some cases, you may want to remodel to allow easier access and care for your child, from adding an extra room to rearranging living areas for safety and ease of navigation. You may need to install ramps to accommodate a wheelchair, grab bars in the bathroom, and or replace a stove with front controls that may be in the reach of a seven year old with reduced mental capacity.

If you are a licensed foster home and plan to adopt or care for more than one special needs child, your state may have funds available for remodeling or even construction. Private agencies often have simpler application forms and quicker response times, so check these out, too.

Dealing with Disabilities

Most parents agree that physical handicaps are the easiest to deal with because they're visible. When you go to the grocery store with a child who rides in a specially equipped wheelchair, and whose problem is obvious, you may get stares, but most reactions will be sympathetic.

Emotional and behavioral disabilities are more difficult for people to understand. They may see your child and wrongly assume you are a bad parent or that you allow your child to behave in an inappropriate way. You must remember that you understand your child's abilities and challenges and others cannot. Hold your head high and ignore the opinions of those who do not understand.

Coping with Nosiness

People are curious, so the middle-aged lady behind you in line at the grocery store may ask what happened to wither your child's legs or take his eyesight. If you are in a check-out line or waiting for a seat at a restaurant, you have no obligation to satisfy anybody's curiosity. You can simply smile and say, "Why do you ask?" Most people won't push the issue.

If a child asks, you probably should give some sort of response that won't invade the privacy of your own child but will educate the child about people with differences. You might say, "He can't talk, but he can see your smile" or "His eyes were hurt in an accident, so he can't see that pretty shirt you're wearing." If your child is verbal and old enough to speak for himself, rehearse with him what he might say to another child who asks questions.

Emotional Disorders

If your child has an emotional disorder, which may also be part of a cluster of disorders, you must know what's happening in your child's brain, and you must find medical and psychological help.

How Your Child's Brain Develops

While brain development starts shortly after conception, it accelerates after birth and continues rapidly until adulthood. The most important time is during the first twelve to fifteen months of life. Immediately after birth, a baby's brain produces trillions more connections than it can possibly use, then begins to eliminate connections for those that are unused. Understanding this concept will help you know how to deal with your child's special needs.

Common Disorders and Causes

Emotional disorders that are very common in adopted foster children are fetal alcohol syndrome (FAS) or fetal alcohol affect (FAA), attention deficit and hyperactivity disorder (ADHD), and reactive attachment disorder (RAD). You must be prepared to deal with these kinds of problems in a very practical way. Wishing them away won't be helpful; neither will the mindset that love conquers all.

Most mental/emotional disorders have a significant biological component. FAS and FAA occur because alcohol ingested by the birth mother affects the fetal brain at all stages of development.

ADHD is a neurobehavioral disorder characterized by inattention, restlessness, and poor impulse control. It is considered to have a genetic link and is the most commonly diagnosed childhood psychiatric disorder. It can also be linked to environment, such as prenatal drug or alcohol exposure, low birth weight, and prenatal smoking.

RAD is a disorder in which a child behaves inappropriately in relationships, especially toward adults in caregiver roles, and is caused by a failure to form healthy attachments to early childhood caregivers.

Resources

Some good places to start finding resources for help with particular problems are the National Alliance for Autism Research at *www .autismspeaks.org* or *www.futurehorizonsautism.com*, *www.reeces rainbow.com*, *www.adoptionBLOGS.com*, *www.AdoptionMedia.com*, and Adoption-Link.org.

You will find parents writing about their experiences, agencies offering help, and advertisers trying to get money out of you. Advertisers are necessary, because they generate the funds to keep the Web sites and blogs open, but be selective in what information you take seriously. See Appendices A and B for lists of where to go for support and education.

Education

Every child in the country has the right to an education geared to his unique needs. School districts implement an individual education plan, or IEP, required by the federal Individuals with Disabilities Education Act. You, as his parent, have a right to participate in the creation of this plan and any adjustments that are made to it later. Talk to your agency and social worker; keep the lines of communication open. Find out as much as possible about your son's school experiences before his placement and read his medical records to see what professionals determined were his best options.

Alert!

Don't be too swayed by a professional's prediction of success. Many parents chuckle over the delight they've found in seeing their children surpass the expectations of experts who merely saw the psychological and intellectual aspects and didn't take into account what loving, dedicated parents, along with supportive siblings, relatives, and therapeutic services, could do for a child's success.

Meet with your local school administrators before enrolling your child. During the first months after placement, visit the classroom often, unannounced, for brief periods of time. If appropriate, make these visits without your child knowing you are there, so you don't interrupt his normal day. Ask for frequent updates from the teachers.

Finding Assistance

You may need to hire a special education attorney who is experienced in working through the system and making sure your child gets every bit of attention and education he is entitled to. School districts want to educate children, but they also must conserve funds. Your attorney will be there to advocate solely for your child and make sure his needs are met.

Most schools have parent organizations for the parents of special needs children. This organization can be very helpful to you. The other parents can explain how the system works and offer advice about how to get the things your child needs.

Dealing with Your Emotions

While knowledge will help you understand why your child behaves as she does, you and the rest of your nuclear family will face issues and have feelings that must be considered. If you don't deal with your emotions, they may cause you to become depressed and unable to meet your child's needs. Other family members could be at risk, too.

When the child you love refuses affection, defies your authority, or screams herself to sleep every night, your feelings will be hurt, and you may become angry. You must stay calm and learn to deal with frustration and anger in positive ways. It can be very overwhelming to suddenly be the main caretaker for a child who needs intensive attention and care. You may feel frightened about what outcomes await her or worried that you simply aren't up to the task. Other family members may share the same worries.

Talk about your feelings with your spouse or close family members. Remember that no feeling is wrong—everything you feel in this situation is valid. It is essential that whatever negative feelings begin to develop in stressful situations, you model appropriate ways to express those feelings.

Reducing Your Stress

While you cannot control your child's behavior or people's reactions around you, you can take steps to help your body relax. Experts in life skills (also known as life coaches or motivational speakers) advise you to stop four or five times a day for five minutes at a time. By stopping, they mean that you should sit down and put your feet up, emptying your mind. If you believe in a higher power, spend at least one set of five minutes praying or connecting to that higher power. If you're afraid you'll distract yourself for too long and get more stressed because you think you're falling further behind, set a timer. Experienced adoptive parents recommend the five-minute break and a nap. Try the following stress busters:

- Take your first break as soon as you get up—set your alarm five minutes early.
- Depending on how much effort is involved in dressing everyone and readying your family for the day, take your next break right after you arrive at work or return from car pooling.
- If possible, take a nap when your child is asleep.
- Take another five minutes after work or when your children are doing homework.
- Wind down your day by devoting some time to yourself just before bed.

Taking the time to de-stress yourself will have positive payoffs for you and your family.

Helping Family Members Cope

You may need to help your children understand that their sibling's behavior may be irritating, embarrassing, or hard to comprehend.

Let them know that feeling anger is normal, but that they must be careful about how they express that anger and that there are good and bad ways to do so. While they have a right to their feelings, their sibling has a right not to be hurt emotionally.

The following are examples of hurtful expressions of anger, with a better, clearer statement after it:

- "Get out of here!"/"My friends and I are playing a game; I'll play with you later."
- "Stop it; don't be so dumb!"/"I don't like to be poked or tickled when I'm trying to read."
- "Why are you so stupid?"/"Maybe we should try doing the puzzle together another time."

Sometimes, children need help finding the right words to convey what they mean in a way that is less hurtful.

Alert!

You must interact with your child at his developmental age. Your adopted child may chronologically be ten years old, but have the cognitive abilities of a five-year-old. Your teenager may have the body of an adult, but react to situations like a three-year-old. Be sure to take that into account in your interactions.

Discuss with your children that there may be times when they will be unsure of how to act around their new sibling. Perhaps your younger child will be embarrassed to have his older, Down syndrome sister insist on playing dolls with him when his best friend from down the street is visiting. Try to be sensitive to such situations; maybe you can take the big sister to another part of the house and play dolls with her yourself. Or take her on a walk to collect pretty leaves or to look for interesting rocks.

Most of all, give your other child individual time to talk about possible scenarios. Tell her it's okay to want to play with her friend without her sister involved, but sometimes she should include her sister.

Helping Your Intellectually or Emotionally Challenged Child

Mental and learning disabilities have multiple causes and diagnosis and can range from slight to complete debilitation. You can't control your child's behavior or perceptions because of his diminished capacities, but you can teach him coping skills and adaptations. Generally, your teaching should be under the direction of medical and psychiatric professionals with experience in your child's particular problem area.

Understanding Your Child's Frames of Reference

Your child does not perceive the world in the same way you do. If you understand what's going on inside his brain, you will be more able to help him.

Time is one of the most difficult concepts for a special needs child to process. A few minutes can seem like hours and a few hours like minutes. Use calendars, digital clocks, and wind-up timers to track days, hours, and minutes. Work with your child to help him figure out what is possible in a minute, five minutes, or an hour. Help him see how time works and why it's important to pay attention to it.

Another common problem is understanding sequencing—why some things have to be first and others follow. When you teach your child a new skill, demonstrate all of the steps. For instance, in assembling a salad: First, you take the ingredients out of the refrigerator and cupboards (you may have to be even more basic and teach what refrigerators and cupboards are for). Then, go through the steps of breaking up the lettuce, slicing the tomatoes, and dicing the onions

Toss the ingredients together and transfer them to a serving bowl and place the bowl on the table.

 Essential

> There are special needs children awaiting international adoption as well as domestic adoption. According to the agency Adoption Associates, 70 percent of the children waiting to be adopted from China have special needs.

Repeat this process for a couple of days in a row, then have him toss the ingredients, transfer them to a serving bowl, and place the bowl on the table. Gradually, move backward until he's able to take the ingredients out of the refrigerator, progress to breaking up the lettuce, and so on, and completing the process by putting the bowl on the table.

Some children need constant repetition before they can master simple reading or math skills. Work closely with your child's teacher, so you can reinforce at home what's being taught in school.

Finding Support

Your child's condition is challenging, and you need support from family, friends, and experts. Remember, however, that whatever advice you receive from your support group should be evaluated according to your instincts and understanding of your child. Consider whether or not the advice seems helpful or harmful. The Internet brings every kind of idea right to your fingertips; your great challenge will be sorting it out.

Elements of a Support Group

The best support groups are those with family situations resembling yours. If you have ethnically different children, then you need other families who are in the same situation. If your child is visually or hearing impaired, you need to be able to talk to parents whose children cannot see or hear well. The same goes for those with emotional or intellectual impairments.

You must be able to share the frustrations and compare strategies. But finding your group can be difficult—you will need to try various methods. Start with your agency and social services in your community. Go to your child's school and talk to the teachers and administrators, especially resource teachers who travel to different schools. Consider placing information in your local newspaper.

 **Alert!**

According to the Center for Adoption Research, adoption of special needs children continues to rise. Adoption of children with medical conditions or disabilities rose from 13.6 percent in 1996 to 24.3 percent in 2003.

If you can't find an established group, organize one yourself. Here, again, your local newspaper can be a great help; enlist the interest and efforts of the editor. You can provide information to a reporter and find other adoptive families. Stay focused and positive, read books, put up flyers on community boards at the grocery store or library.

Supplement your local group with online support. Literally hundreds of blogs and Web sites are at your fingertips. Just type in "autism support group," "oppositional defiance disorder," or "low vision," and you'll be amazed by what comes up. Because there is so much information now on the Internet, remember that many things you might read about your child's disability could be inaccurate. Parenting suggestions can also be confusing. It is best to take information you find and work on verifying it through more direct means by working closely with a therapeutic service provider, doctor, or local support group of a national association focused on your child's disability.

Support from Family and Friends

Reach out to your family, neighbors, and friends. Ask a friend to play chess with your wheelchair-bound daughter while you take a couple of hours to get your hair cut and browse the new arrivals at the library. Let your mother know that you'd like an overnight get-away with your spouse. If limited funds put a hotel out of reach, see if she'll take your child so you can have private time in your own house.

Adopting a mentally or physically disabled child changes the dynamics of your extended family. Your grandparents, uncles and aunts, and cousins may worry about your own physical and mental health, especially if they have little or no experience with autism, ADHD, cerebral palsy, or other problems and disorders. You will have to educate them, while reminding them that you knew what you were getting into. Explain that their support and help is important and that you would appreciate their acceptance of your choices.

Most of the time, a little education is all you need. Those who love you the most can give you the most. However, do remember that, ultimately, you cannot control people's emotions. If your parents or siblings react negatively to your daughter who has autism, limit contact, because your daughter's emotional needs have priority.

Focus on What's Most Important

As described in other parts of this book and earlier in this chapter, acknowledge that you are working on a cause that transcends the ordinary. Extraordinary results come from sustained, consistent actions. But you can do nothing if you let yourself become exhausted, anxious, and depleted. Instead, stay focused on the joy your new child has brought to your life and the difference you have been able to make in hers.

CHAPTER 13

Dynamics of Biological and Adoptive Relationships

Your child had parents before he came into your life, even if you took him home from the hospital at birth. Because he had other parents, but now has you, he has a duality situation that can be confusing. Learning how to talk about and manage relationships with birth families is one of the biggest challenges of adoption.

Different Types of Adoptions Meet Different Needs

The type of adoption you choose will impact the kind of relationship you and your child will have with members of her birth family. The key to any successful adoption is making sure that your child understands who her primary family is. Children must attach to a primary family, whether that family is biological or adoptive, in order to grow up emotionally healthy. They can love and relate to lots of extended family and friends, but they must have only one main family. At the same time that your child attaches to your family, she can maintain a connection to her birth family.

Current research, including the Minnesota-Texas Adoption Research Project (MTARP) that tracked 190 adoptive families and 169 birth mothers from 1987 to 2000, found that the best results between birth and adoptive families happened when the families negotiated their relationship early in the process, with the help of their agencies. Once the boundaries were established, the adoptive parents managed the contact during early and late childhood, then shifted the responsibility for initiating and maintaining contact to adolescents approaching adulthood. And, finally, adult adoptees continued contact, or not, according to their specific choices.

 Fact

> The Minnesota-Texas Adoption Research Project study indicated that one type of adoption arrangement isn't always better than another. Researchers have determined that one-size-fits-all legislation about open or closed adoptions should not be enacted because of the multiple varieties and combinations that exist among families formed by adoption.

Understand Birth Parent Grief

All adoptions start with a loss by the birth parents, either voluntarily or mandated by the courts, so emotions can run high. Adoptive mothers interviewed for this book describe how hard it was for them to watch the birth mothers struggle and grieve as they signed the papers. Seeing the pain of the women who were responsible for their own joy was difficult to endure. They expressed how hard it was to contain their own joy and how conflicted it felt to know that joy was built on another's pain. Because of this grief, many birth parents decide to go with an open adoption, so they don't lose touch. Sometimes it works and sometimes it doesn't.

Dealing with Jealousy

It is normal to have jealous feelings toward your child's birth mother or father. You may be jealous of any mother who could conceive while you couldn't. Even if you chose to adopt rather than have a biological child for personal reasons, you may still feel jealousy toward any person who has a birth family claim on your child.

While your feelings are normal, they can also get in the way of your parenting, so you must recognize and deal with them. The best results for you and your child will happen when you and the birth family agree and work together for the benefit of everybody involved.

Grieving to Overcome Jealousy

To overcome your jealousy, you may need to deal with some grief issues. First, you need to grieve over not having given birth to your child. Maybe you endured years of infertility and sorrow over never experiencing pregnancy or over pregnancy loss. Perhaps you already have a biological child but suffered secondary infertility. Whatever your circumstances, remember that it's normal to wish you'd given birth to your child. But as an emotionally healthy person, you will work through the stages of grief (see Chapter 7 for information about the stages of grief) and arrive at a point where you will find joy in the family you build.

Second, your child needs to go through the same process, although an infant or young child will express grief very differently from an older child or adolescent. Acknowledging his grief will help you attach to your child. He will have to grieve to put to rest the emotional realities that come with losing his original set of parents. You can't make it all better no matter how much you love him, but you can be the steady foundation on which he will build the rest of his life.

Alert!

Nancy, a New Jersey adoptive mom, is frustrated when the birth mom calls or comes over whenever she feels like it. Nancy's biggest problem is that the birth mom still thinks she can tell Nancy and her husband how to parent. "They (the birth parents) both want to keep the mommy and daddy title but do NONE of the work. They just don't get it." Setting boundaries from the start is the best way to avoid this kind of problem.

The birth parents and their families will also endure a grieving process, but don't get sidetracked into taking responsibility for their behavior and emotions. You can be caring, even supportive, but your first allegiance is to your own family.

Dealing with Chance Encounters

Whether or not you are in an open adoption, you will have to consider how to respond if you or your child is contacted outside the parameters of the adoption agreement. Contact can range from chance meetings in the grocery store to intrusive or secret phone calls and unwanted visits.

Imagine yourself sitting in the doctor's office with your toddler whom you adopted two weeks ago. A woman approaches you, saying, "That's my sister's baby! I'd know her anywhere." Then the woman bends down and reaches for your daughter. Your daughter stares at her and shrinks against your thigh. How do you respond? The woman obviously knows your child, but you have been told by social services that contact with the biological family is forbidden.

Your first concern is protecting your child, emotionally and physically, so try not to be confrontational, but state that you are not going to discuss the situation. Put your arms around your child and lift her into your lap. Be gentle and firm; if the woman doesn't move away or insists on continuing the conversation, pick up your daughter and walk to the reception desk.

Chance encounters are going to happen, unless you live on opposite sides of the country. Even then, mass transportation means that you can't guarantee avoiding contact altogether. If your adoption is closed, respond politely and without rancor when you run into a birth family member. If your child is old enough to know what's going on, be sure to talk to her after the encounter. Experienced adoptive parents suggest the following tactics:

- **Age five and younger**—Observe your child's behavior during and after the experience. If she acts anxious or clingy, say, "Did seeing that lady scare you?" Then say, "I'm sorry you were upset. I'm right here," and spend extra time cuddling or whatever she needs.
- **Ages six to twelve**—Depending on your child's mental age, you can talk about whether she remembers the person and exactly what those memories are. Gently try to help her articulate her feelings, validate them, and remind her that you are her parent and will keep her safe.
- **Ages thirteen and up**—Younger teens may need you to reassure them that toxic people from their previous life will not be able to hurt them. If serious abuse has occurred, seeing someone from the biological family can trigger trauma response in your child. In these cases, you most likely need to work with a therapist who will guide you about just what you should say.

If you're in an open adoption, you should respond as you would with any member of your extended family. Exchange greetings and light conversation, then excuse yourself and get on with what you were doing. If the behavior by the birth family member is not appropriate, get out of the situation as quickly as possible in a polite yet firm way.

Create a Feeling of Safety

An adopted child's greatest fear is that those who are supposed to love and care for him will disappear. For many children adopted from foster care or internationally, this fear has become reality in the past. Safety is more than physical safety—it pertains to emotions as well.

Your primary purpose is to develop attachments between your child and you, your partner or spouse, and other children in the family. To do so, you need accurate information about your child's prenatal and early experiences, so you can understand behavior in context. You need to know what has happened in the past so you can make plans about how to handle the future.

Boundaries for Birth Families

If your child's birth family is going to be involved in your child's life (if you've adopted a relative's child or a stepchild or signed an open adoption agreement), you and they must agree on boundaries that will facilitate attachment for you and your child. An open or kinship adoption is not a coparenting arrangement. There should be no doubt about who is the parent and who is an important adult in the child's life.

Most experienced adoptive parents describe the birth mother or father's role in a completely open adoption as similar to that of an aunt or uncle. You have the right to parent according to your own values and style, without interference from the birth family. The birth family is there to provide some extra love and attention for your child, but is not involved in day-to-day parenting.

Teaching about How Your Family Functions

If your child is a toddler or older when adopted, he will probably have experienced at least one devastating loss and maybe several. Because of this, you will need to use concrete methods for teaching your child how your family functions and that it is a safe place.

It can be helpful to be as visual as possible, as well as repetitive, as you teach your child what it means to be in your family. Make a poster with pictures of everybody in the family. Put your picture and your spouse's at the top. Then write "Mom and Dad set the rules, provide the food, and give love" under your pictures. You can write similar statements for each sibling and your child or use words on the poster such as "Everybody will be safe in our family," "We eat together and share hugs," "We all have jobs to do," and so on.

You will probably have to verbalize such things as, "Daddy goes to work to get money to buy food and he always comes home again" or "Big people do not hurt children in our family." You will have to say these things over and over again, probably for months or even years.

 Essential

If you are interested in learning about the effect of adoption on birth mothers, read *Birthmothers: Women Who Have Relinquished Babies for Adoption Tell Their Stories* by Merry Block Jones.

Questions and Concerns about the Birth Family

Your child will have all sorts of questions about her first family. Curiosity varies with each child, but all children wonder about where they came from and why they're not with those people anymore.

Sometimes this curiosity is brief, especially between the ages of six and twelve, but children approaching the teen years will usually bring the questions to the forefront. Prepare ahead of time. Be fully educated about your child's biological parents and extended family. Make notes about your experiences searching for information for your child; also, copy documents or placement papers. Keep the information in a readily accessible place. Be prepared to answer questions in an age-appropriate manner.

Understanding Birth Mother Emotional Paradoxes

Explain to your child that her birth mother endured conflicting emotions as she struggled to figure out what was best for her and for herself. If your child is young, tailor your explanation to what she can understand. She needs to know that she was not responsible, in any way, for being given up for adoption. Assure her that her biological parents could not raise her, but loved her enough to find a wonderful home for her. Tell her that you are her parent in every way and she's yours forever and ever.

When your child reaches adolescence, tell her that many birth mothers are caught up in a paradox. If they keep their children, they face financial and emotional hurdles, especially if they're very young, single, or if the birth father isn't involved. Raising a child is challenging at best, as any parent will testify, and it's even more so when done solo.

Many mothers find that they don't have the emotional or financial resources to support themselves and a child. Yet, they fear the reactions of their friends and family if they choose adoption. If they just leave their children with somebody and don't come back, they're often prosecuted and can go to jail.

Children who are adopted internationally should be helped to understand that birth mothers from their country of origin often face tremendous poverty, stress, and difficult living conditions, and that these factors played out against the mother's deep love for her baby.

 Essential

Adolescence is a volatile time for any child, so your teen might tell you she wants to live with her biological family, instead of you. Don't be drawn into a fight. Your child can't "unadopt" herself. Even though older teens are able to become legally emancipated, it is more helpful to find ways to keep giving your teen structure and guidance while allowing more freedom and responsibilities within the family home.

Help your child understand the paradoxes birth mothers face. Explain that decisions were made and actions taken based on love and the best intentions of everybody involved. Reinforce the permanency of your family bond.

Unlawful Contact from the Birth Family

If birth family members initiate contact when you have a closed adoption or when the contact initiated falls outside of the terms of the adoption agreement, it can be stressful for you and difficult for your child, depending on his age and the exact circumstances. Unlawful contact usually occurs when parental rights have been terminated for cause by the state.

For example, Lanie and Jerry adopted Marnie through the foster care system when she was ten and Dale, as an infant, through a private arrangement. When Marnie was fourteen, her birth mother spotted Marnie in front of the local high school and approached her. Terrified, Marnie ran inside the school and called Lanie. After dinner that night Marnie paced the room, shaking her fist and raging about the incident. Her little brother couldn't understand why she was so upset, since he enjoyed seeing his birth mother. Lanie and Jerry explained that Marnie was angry because her birth mother didn't follow the rules, but that they would protect her. Marnie and Jerry contacted the agency and alerted them to the situation.

Responding to Unwanted Contact

Unwanted contact can range from somebody breaking the visitation rules to outright stalking by members of the birth family. Be careful not to lose your temper or say anything derogatory about the person involved in front of your child. Make sure you react according to your legal agreement.

If you start receiving phone calls in the middle of the night from the birth mom, when you'd agreed to only have contact via the agency, you should immediately call your agency, because the legal terms have been violated. While you may empathize with her, remember that neither her feelings nor yours are as important as the attachment and safety of your child.

If the birth mother shows up on your doorstep without arranging an appointment, you can insist that she come back later at your convenience. If the agreement you originally negotiated doesn't seem to be working, renegotiate it, but understand that you, the legal parent, have the right and responsibility to decide who does or does not see your child, and under what circumstances.

Extended Birth Family Visitation Rights

Although birth parents have relinquished their rights or had those rights terminated by the state, your child may have relatives who don't want to lose contact. Frequently, grandparents or uncles and aunts may have cared for your child and established bonds with her. These people can be important support and a source of reassurance for your child and you.

Responding to Requests for Visitation

If you are contacted by a biological relative, you must first check with your agency (or whoever facilitated your adoption) to find out what your obligations are. In most cases, you don't have any legal obligations to allow access to your child.

Guided by your agency, find out exactly what the relationship was and whether or not there is any reason to limit contact. Today, kinship placements are usually sought before a child is released for adoption, so perhaps home studies took place or family members were asked to take the child and couldn't. Get the specifics so you can plan appropriately.

Usually, extended family will welcome contact within the boundaries you set. Few children can have too many people who love them. Be vigilant, especially during the years when your child is young, and avoid overnight or unsupervised visits. Trust your instincts and help your child learn to process her own emotions.

Different Types of Family Bonds

Families today are complicated. Some pundits joke about family "bushes" rather than family "trees." Divorces and remarriages, as well as kinship adoptions and open adoptions, can be very confusing to young children. While adults have the reasoning capacity to understand different levels of relationships, children may get lost in trying to navigate those levels.

Adopted children may have stepparents, grandparents, and cousins. They may have siblings from the same mother and father or from different mothers and fathers. The siblings may have lived together for awhile or been in different households. Your child may have formed a sibling attachment with other children in her foster home. Or your child may acquire a sibling after being adopted.

 *Question?*

How can I answer my child when she asks what her birth family looks like when I really don't know?
Show her pictures of your birth relatives who have similar features and coloring to you and tell her that genes passed by parents determine what people look like. Then stand with her in front of a mirror and talk about the coloring and features that her birth family may share based upon the characteristics of herself that she sees in the mirror.

All of these relationships will have an impact on her. Be as open and accepting as possible as you explore her feelings with her. This openness will help her understand her emotions and how they change as she grows up.

Be alert to your child's fears, uncertainties, or resistance to interacting with birth family members. Although you don't want to be unduly suspicious, always trust your parental instincts. Talk to a therapist or someone objective if you find yourself growing more concerned over time.

Separated Siblings

Siblings are closer genetically than parents and children. Relationships can be especially strong in dysfunctional families where siblings took care of each other. Find out just what kind of sibling bond your child had. That knowledge will dictate what kind of contact you allow, as well as the frequency and location of visits. You might find it helpful to support sibling contact if they trust and enjoy each other's company. You might also find it necessary to limit contact between siblings if your child was overly responsible for his sibling or overcontrolled by his sibling acting in a parental role with him.

Benefits of Placing Siblings Together

Your child may share a history with his sibling. If the brother or sister is older, that child can help the younger one understand the dynamics that led to the separation and help fill in gaps for memory books and therapy. If your child came from an abusive or neglectful home, the sibling bonds will be stronger than the attachments to their parents. Therefore, having each other could lessen the trauma of separation from their parents.

Importance of Sibling Bonds

Agencies work with the rule that siblings should be placed in the same home if they've lived together or have more than a casual bond. Some cannot be placed together because of the size of the family. It can be difficult to find adoptive homes able to take more than two or three siblings. Obviously, if a sibling abused a brother or sister or if there was some other toxic element to the relationship, placement in the same house would not be appropriate. If placement isn't possible because of health or other issues, then every effort should be made to ensure an ongoing relationship if that relationship would be beneficial.

Strategies for Promoting Sibling Bonds

If your child has siblings who are not in your home, you can help establish and maintain ties. Consider your child's age and whether or not a relationship existed previously before you decide just what type of contact and how much to encourage. Toddlers and preschoolers who have no memory of a sibling will just be confused if you introduce an unknown sibling who doesn't live with you. Wait until your child is in elementary school before springing the news.

 Essential

> If you know your child has a sibling but you can't have contact or don't know where she is, help your child make a Sister's or Brother's Box which can contain drawings, pictures, and small gifts. Occasionally get the box out and add to it. At some point, your child will probably want contact, but maybe not until he's grown.

Once you and your child know about the existence of a sibling and your child is old enough to understand, don't wait for your child to request contact. Depending on where the sibling lives, try to arrange for face-to-face visits as frequently as possible. Use technology, the phone, instant messaging, and so on (but be sure you monitor the calls or messages, so nothing inappropriate takes place).

Invite siblings to special events like birthdays, sports tournaments, school activities, and holidays. Keep pictures of the siblings with other pictures of members of your family.

Maintaining a relationship with a sibling means that you will have to maintain contact with the sibling's family. The sibling might live with your child's birth parents, or may have been placed in an adoptive or foster home. You will need to develop a cooperative relationship with the parents to ensure that visits do happen and that they happen smoothly. If your child's birth parents are not permitted to have contact, it may be difficult to arrange visitation with a sibling who still lives with the birth parents. Discuss the possibilities with your agency.

CHAPTER 14

Emotional Pitfalls for
Adopted Children

As the parent of an adopted child, you not only must have basic parenting skills, you must be able to meet the needs of a child who has a different biological origin. In addition to the usual needs and frustrations of any growing child, your adopted child also worries about her place in the family and wonders about birth parents. It is important to remember that no child is perfect, and any child is likely to experience phases that involve emotional distress. As an adoptive parent, you need to be on the lookout for normal problems that escalate into situations that require help.

Confronting Feelings of Abandonment and Emotional Trauma

Your child's emotional reactions will depend on whether she's a young infant or older, whether she's from another country or different racial group, and whether you have other children already. Your essential tasks are to thoughtfully and carefully figure out just what you can do to heal past traumas, to engage your child in the reality of where she is, and to support and promote a secure attachment to you, so that she will grow up emotionally and mentally healthy.

Importance of Attachment
If you brought your child home from the hospital or adopted her within a few weeks of birth, your child will, in general, have

few problems with feelings of desertion. But once your child is old enough to understand biological relationships, the questions will start, and emotions will become complicated. Feelings of abandonment are lessened and finally eradicated as your child progresses through the stages of attachment that begin at birth.

A child who has not developed healthy attachments to caregivers may respond with these kinds of behaviors:

- Cruelty to others and pets
- Lack of long-term friends
- Superficial and indiscriminate friendliness, especially toward strangers
- Lack of eye contact and resistance to nurturing touch

Attachment doesn't happen all at once. It's a long-term process that continues and changes over time. It consists of approximately five to seven stages (depending on how the levels of intimacy are broken down). Each stage must be accomplished before your child can move to the next.

The first three stages, Learning to Trust, Learning about Family, and Developing Autonomy, occur during infancy and early childhood. The next stage, Learning about Social Roles, is a transitional stage that allows your child to prepare for relationships outside your family and needs to happen for her to succeed in school. The final stage of attachment, Developing Independence and Competency, starts around age twelve (but can happen as early as eight or nine) and continues through the teens.

Promoting Attachment in Infants

Stage One, Learning to Trust, is the most critical of all, because it should begin immediately after birth and usually end within six months if outside circumstances don't come into play. Unfortunately, a significant number of adoptable children don't have the opportunity to enter and progress through this stage. If they never do, they can become emotionally impaired, developing relationships that are unsuccessful and often never experiencing the rewards of true intimacy.

Your baby must learn that you are reliable and can be trusted to meet her needs. Through you, she'll learn the world is a safe place for her. Your baby also learns that she can get you to respond to her by using attachment cues (e.g., crying when hungry) to express she needs something. Over time and with thousands of repetitions of expressing needs and getting them met, this intricate exchange of attachment cues between you and your baby helps her develop the belief that she is capable and lovable.

People watching the interchange of attachment cues and responses between a baby and primary caregiver often liken it to a dance. If your baby doesn't come to you until she is several months old, she will either have attached to a previous primary caregiver or she may have been neglected by a birth parent or institution and be emotionally fragile, and weak in successfully using attachment cues.

 Fact

Your pediatrician can give you specifics, but in general your baby needs an iron-fortified formula with licopene for her first year. Commercial formulas contain balanced proteins, fats, carbohydrates, sugars, vitamins, and minerals necessary to sustain rapid growth. Neglected infants will need more specialized diets, based on medical knowledge about nutrients they may have missed.

If your baby has already made an attachment, she must transfer that attachment to you, a process that takes some time. Her grief at the separation from her previous caregiver will be more intense if her first caregiver doesn't absolutely agree to you being the parent. This can be a major factor when the state steps in and removes a child from birth parents.

Her foster parent or primary caregiver can help her feel safe by giving her permission to become your child. Of course, your baby can't understand spoken language, nor can she speak, but she can understand or sense the emotions of those around her.

Help your baby complete Stage One by:

- Providing a predictable environment
- Responding to her cues about hunger, discomfort, and fear
- Playing with her and responding to her vocalizations and gestures
- Initiating eye and skin-to-skin contact
- Rocking her and talking to her during feedings
- Helping her learn to self-soothe

It's important that the person who has cared for her clearly and vocally tell her it's okay to trust you and that you will be her parent. This transition of trust can take place in a variety of ways. For instance, take over feeding, diapering, or bathing after the foster mom starts the process. Do this for a few times, then respond to your baby's needs while the foster mom watches, and finally, respond without her present. Some babies will transition more easily than others. Get help from your pediatrician or social worker if things become too hard.

Promoting Attachment in Toddlers

Toddlers (children between the ages of twelve and thirty-six months) have the most difficult time changing caregivers because their verbal and cognitive skills are limited, yet they are very aware of their surroundings and sensitive to change. They tend to get stuck, as many therapists describe it, in this early phase of attachment. You will need to replicate, as much as possible, the care needed at the early phase of attachment she is stuck in. For example, she may have been swaddled tightly at nighttime, an activity that signals it's time for sleep. If you think she's too old for such swaddling, gradually loosen the blankets over a period of days or weeks until she can fall asleep in response to your specific cues.

If your baby spent eighteen months in an orphanage and was handed a bottle or food to give to herself, you will have to take back the feeding role, gently and consistently. If your toddler was abused as well as neglected, you will need serious psychological intervention and the guidance of a therapist or pediatrician who specializes in attachment and complicated trauma.

Progression Issues

Unless your child has completed the first stage of the attachment process, she will be unable to move into Stage Two. If she's been neglected and or abused, her brain chemistry will have her on high alert and she won't be able to relax enough to relate to you.

 **Fact**

The second level of attachment, Learning about Family, normally takes place when your child is between six and eighteen months of age. Babies in this stage often demonstrate stranger anxiety. They turn to Mom or Dad, whom they trust, to keep them safe when they're afraid. They learn who is family and who is not, and test the boundaries of those relationships.

You may find that your child will resist your touch and she may be stiff and fearful. Her respiration and heart rate may accelerate and she may shut down emotionally. Shutting down is a protective mechanism for children who have no power over what happens to them. Other protective mechanisms are punching, running, spitting, or biting. You have to get past the fear response before anything positive can happen. Your primary task will be to complete the Stage One process, starting with where she's stuck, and that will be different for each child.

Attachment Issues for Older Children

If your child is a tween or teen when you adopt her, your obstacles may seem huge because you will also be dealing with the normal challenges that come with the adolescent's desire for more separation and independence from parents. An adolescent who hasn't securely attached has the added sorrow of knowing what she's missed. She may have been harmed by the emotional and physical trauma of growing up in a dangerous environment, where she always had to be on alert or where she left the frightening circumstances behind by disconnecting. See Chapter 10 for more information.

Alert!

Two books with excellent suggestions for building secure attachments at each stage are *The Connected Child* by Dr. Karyn Purvis and *Attaching in Adoption* by Deborah D. Gray. For serious situations, reading alone won't be enough—you'll need the help of an attachment therapist who specializes in adoption.

Preadolescence is a significant time for your child to question her identity. The last two stages of attachment (Learning about Social Roles and Developing Independence) are when children figure out relationships to their peers and discover their adult identities. These last two stages allow them to move from the safety of your home into establishing their own families, but adoption makes the process more difficult. Your child will have an added struggle due to her adoption and separation from her birth family. This can be a time when your child does not fully understand the desire to separate from you.

On some level, separating from home reminds her of her first painful separation from her biological family. If her adoption experience has not been openly talked about through her developing years, she may feel confused and ambivalent about leaving home, not being able to make the distinction between bad or painful separations and leaving with the excitement of exploring a new phase of her life.

Special Issues Stemming from Lack of Attachment

If you have a vision in your head of a child who responds to your overtures with hugs and delighted laughter, you may be crushed when your child turns her back and ignores you—or worse, yells that she hates you. Unattached children are not gratifying for parents; they don't know how to reciprocate kind words and actions. It takes many months, often years, for them to learn this essential human skill.

You will be challenged to change mindsets and concepts your child learned at a preverbal level. A child who never received nurturing interaction as an infant will feel neglected and may act out no matter how much attention she receives now.

If you have an anxious child, don't make the mistake of mirroring that anxiety. You should take advantage of your greater knowledge and de-stress yourself. The more needy your child is, the greater your stress levels will be. It's imperative that you find ways to lower your stress, so you can maintain your high-structure/high-nurturing parenting.

Methods for Changing Behavior

If your child is exhibiting behavior that doesn't fit in with your household rules, you need to learn to redirect and change that behavior. If your child acts out because of fear, anger, or other negative impacts of his earlier disruptions, stop tiptoeing around him, waiting for the next outburst. You should be setting the tone in your home—that's not your child's role. Don't make the mistake of taking responsibility for your child's pain. You can't; you can only redirect your child's behavior and reinforce the fact that he's safe with you.

If your child's behavior begins to spiral out of control, try to disrupt the meltdown before it escalates. This technique requires you to be nearby and aware. Distract him with a gentle touch and comment: "Let's read the Bunny book." Offer a snack or a drink of water.

Say something slightly odd or humorous to get his attention. Use your imagination to shift his attention to something less emotionally laden, activating the use of a different section of his brain where troubling memories and intense emotions aren't stored.

If things have progressed too quickly and are beyond your ability to distract, give a "time in," where you restrict your son to his mad place, such as a chair in the kitchen while you work nearby, or the family room couch. When your child is calm, help him practice breathing techniques that he can use when he feels anger or fear coming on. Demonstrate that rapid, shallow breathing and tensed muscles will make him more upset, and that he can slow down his breathing and take control of his feelings. Lead him through taking slow, deep breaths and holding them for a count of five; work your way up to ten.

Peaceful Discipline Tactics

High-structure parenting means that you set boundaries and apply consequences when those boundaries are broken or pushed too far. Your consequences, however, must not be anything that brings up fear of abandonment.

You will be challenged to devise immediate and appropriate consequences for unacceptable behavior, but as you set up the structure, keep in mind the underlying causes of certain behaviors. A child who is afraid will run, bite, kick, and scream. You must help him feel safe before he can let go of his fear and the behavior it prompts.

Next, use logical consequences and "time in" rather than "time out." Keep your child near you as you show him how to clean up the mess he made or figure out a better way of reacting to a mean remark than kicking somebody. See Chapters 13, 16, and 18 for more information.

Dealing with Curiosity and Fantasies

Every child, adopted or not, is curious about where she came from. All children are fascinated by stories and traditions that help them understand their place in the family.

The younger your child was when you adopted her, the more likely she will build up a fantasy about her birth family. In the give and take of normal family life, your child may get upset with you and secretly wish for her "real" mom or dad to come back and rescue her from the boredom of chores or restrictions.

Critical Ages for Fantasies

Fantasies or romantic notions about her birth family start about the time a child reaches school age. This imaginary life is perfectly normal, but of course that doesn't mean you should buy into the fantasy. It's okay to allow your child to have the fantasy; however, you should always answer her questions about her origins honestly. Understanding and acknowledging the confusion and conflicts your child may experience will help you forge a bond.

 Essential

As your child dreams of his "real" parents, who are beautiful, rich, and always indulgent, he will have a hard time reconciling that dream with his knowledge that those parents gave up their child. While a younger child will think he may have been stolen and his birth parents are looking for him, the older child will figure out that probably isn't true.

Your child may say confusing things like, "When I was in your tummy, did I kick a lot?" She's trying to figure out how and why she belongs to you as well as what kind of person she is. Because children have a concrete understanding of the world, making general statements about her as a baby can be helpful. You can say things like, "All babies kick when they're inside their mother's body, so I'm sure you kicked also." Then, you can use such questions or comments to reassure her that she didn't grow in your tummy, but she grew in your heart—which is the most important place of all!

Acknowledging and Strengthening Connections

Most professionals advise that, when possible, you and the birth family conduct a placement ceremony, where you claim the child and the biological parent gives the child permission to be part of your family. When and where this ceremony takes place will depend on your child's age and whether or not the state terminated parental rights.

Naming or renaming your child can be part of the claiming process, but it can also cause some problems. Naming is an important cultural function that establishes a child as a member of the family. If you adopt an infant, naming won't be an issue. If you have an open adoption of an older child, you may want to discuss the name with the birth parents so that any issues over it can be resolved amicably. If your adoption of an older child is closed, you still should avoid changing the first name of a child who has learned to respond to that name.

Alert!

You have the right to change your child's name legally, but be careful about making the change abruptly, especially if the child is more than a month or two old. Also, when your child grows older, he will be more likely to see his name as a link to his birth family, ethnicity, or culture and be sad or upset about losing it.

If you feel strongly that the name should be changed, first incorporate the old name for awhile with the new name, then gradually use the new name more than the old, and eventually phase it out altogether. Do write down why you wanted to change the name and put the information in a place where you can discuss it with your child at the appropriate time.

If you adopt a child from another country, you might wish to incorporate part of her birth name in order to retain a feeling of connection to that heritage. Some parents keep the child's first name as a middle name.

Failed or Disrupted Adoptions

The vast majority of adoptions are successful as permanent placements of a child into a new family. However, there are circumstances in which a happy ending is not possible. Failed adoptions are the most tragic of events—worse for the child, in many psychologists' opinions than death of a parent or divorce. Unfortunately, this tragedy is sometimes unavoidable for many complicated reasons.

Because of the protective mechanisms that children develop in response to neglect and abuse, their behavior can be very difficult to deal with. The older a child is and the greater the number of caregivers he's had, the more it affects the bonding and attachment process when he is adopted. Many parents are stunned by the violent reactions of children they thought would fit into their families.

Children who have missed out on nurturing may fail to attach and get caught in what therapist Deborah Gray calls The Needing to Win/No Win Spiral. These children use anger and manipulation to try to control parents, behavior that can cause parents to be outraged and make them question whether the effort is worth the pain. The chaos and high level of stimulation can actually be addictive to an abused child. As things calm down, your child may intentionally goad you into angry outbursts so that things can seem familiar.

Prevent Failure

Before you move too far into the adoption process, particularly when adopting an older child, be certain that you know what you're getting into. You should receive information about the physical and emotional challenges your child has or will face. It's tempting to see a picture of a child and read a brief description and think, "This kid's for me!" but don't make up your mind before you know all the facts. Do your homework and meet the child in a neutral setting. Then gradually progress to private visits where you can engage the child in play and note his personality and willingness to be open to connection. Even in international adoption, it is usually possible (and often required) that you meet the child first. However, your few brief visits may not be enough to really be able to get to know the child. Get a professional opinion when possible, about the child's behavior and condition. Even with a thorough examination of your prospective child by a number of interested people and professionals, there are psychological difficulties in some children that will not be evident in an evaluative setting or during initial contacts.

Remember that an older child knows what adoption means, although he may have an idealized perception. He could "court" you and be on his best behavior. Listen to your emotional responses as you watch him with your spouse or other children. Try to visit in several different locations, and don't rush into anything. On the other hand, it's not fair to the child for you to take too long to make up your mind. So, if you can't commit for the long term, be honest.

Disruption

Disruption is the term used when a planned adoption does not take place. If you find that the child you were planning to adopt has disabilities or conditions you were unaware of or exhibits behavior you are unable to cope with, disruption is an option. It is better to disrupt an adoption, than to go through with it and then have it fail. Once a child is placed in a permanent home, that home really should be permanent whenever possible. Disruption is painful for everyone involved, but it is a better option than failure.

Alternatives

If you decide after a while that you cannot continue to parent because of danger to yourself or your other children, there are options other than adoption failure. Your adopted child may be too mentally or emotionally ill to live in a normal family. He may need to be hospitalized, then placed in a therapeutic home.

If you didn't find out the depth of the problems your child had until after finalization, you may not have to terminate the adoption after all. You can continue as if the child were your biological child, born to you with a serious mental illness. Your child may not be able to live in your home, but you can still take responsibility for him and be the one who interfaces with doctors, therapists, and others. State laws vary, but you can usually be the parent without assuming the financial responsibility if your circumstances preclude funding his care.

Previous Failures or Disruptions

If your child has suffered a failed adoption or multiple placements before coming to you, he may be convinced that he's worthless. In his mind, if he were worth something, he would not have been rejected.

 Essential

According to *Adoption and Disruptions* by Richard Barth, less than 1 percent of infant adoptions disrupt; 9.7 percent of adoptions of children ages six to twelve disrupt; 13.5 percent of adoptions of children ages twelve to eighteen disrupt; and 14.3 percent of special needs adoptions disrupt.

The emotional problems your child develops from previous rejection, disruption, abuse, and other situations beyond his control are so damaging that they may cause him to fail in his adult relationships without significant effort on your part. You will have to, in the words of Dr. Karyn Purvis, author of *The Connected Child*, "Fill the trust bank." You must repeatedly, over time (which can often seem endless) use gentle touch and loving words such as, "You are my precious son" or "I enjoy just being with you."

Demonstrate your commitment to your child and your belief in his worthiness in everything you do: during dinner when you dish his carrots and cut up his meat, at night as you tuck him into bed with a kiss and a smile, and when he wakes up in the morning to your welcoming hug. All of your actions should reinforce connection to you and the rest of the family.

Being "The Adopted Kid" at School

For some reason, the perception among many teachers and administrators is that being adopted means a child will have more emotional and mental problems than the average child. However, children who are adopted in early childhood are no more likely to have problems than biological children. In most cases, adoption by committed, enlightened parents ameliorates the harm to children who may have been damaged by illness, accident, or toxic parenting.

Deciding Need to Know

You must decide what sort of information your child's school needs to further her education. Here, again, your child's age and circumstances of being placed in your home are the defining factors. A lot will depend on the particular form of your adoption and behaviors that may stem from the situation. If your child was adopted as an infant, the adoption may not be relevant information. If your child is ten years old and was adopted last week, the school will need this information.

The teachers should know enough about your child's background to deal with her and optimize her chances for academic success. Don't share the gory details though. A simple "She was neglected (and or abused) and is afraid much of the time" will suffice. Knowing that your child cannot control her behavior without an adult nearby will allow her teacher to plan how to work with the behavior.

Confronting Special Issues

If your child has fear and past abuse issues, she may not be able to learn easily. She may mask her fears with bravado, being numb, or acting out in a way that causes havoc in the classroom. Her brain has been wired for danger, not learning. It may take years for rewiring to finish.

 Fact

> Your child needs a diet high in protein, complex carbohydrates, fruits, and vegetables, combined with exercise and plenty of sleep, in order for her brain to function at optimum levels. You should avoid feeding her saturated fats and empty calories, but don't cut out unsaturated fats, like fish oil. Check with your pediatrician about a well-rounded diet for your child's age group.

Work with your child's teacher to make her understand that your child needs clear structure and probably won't respond well to having too many choices. She also should be seated close to the teacher, so the teacher can correct inappropriate behavior. In addition, she may need a personal aide who, if prescribed by your therapist, should be provided through the school district.

Testing can be a challenge for children with emotional or learning disabilities. The regular testing that occurs at mandated intervals in schools may not work for your child. You need to go to your school district and request a more direct, thorough approach. This kind of testing usually takes four to six hours and must be administered by a neuropsychologist. Most school systems do not provide testing this thorough.

Involving Mental Health Professionals

At some point, you may want to consult with a therapist, social worker, or pediatrician who has training in adoption issues. Finding a professional who fits your family's needs will take effort and time. Work with your placement agency and or your pediatrician to decide whether your child needs physical therapy, hospitalization, psychiatric intervention, or behavior modification that can be supervised by a therapist.

Deciding What Kind of Help You Need

Trust your instincts and your knowledge of your family and your child. Don't think the worst right away. However, if your child demonstrates any of the following behaviors, immediately contact your agency or social services network in your community:

- Is aggressive and shows no remorse when he hurts someone
- Steals and lies without any apparent reason
- Harms himself
- Refuses affection and isolates himself from the rest of the family

If dealt with early on, these behaviors can be changed, but they can indicate deep psychological problems and shouldn't be ignored.

Impact of the Past

One of your biggest fears may be that your child, if he was removed from the birth family, will repeat his birth parents' behaviors or mistakes. Some people just assume that adopted children are doomed because of the mistakes or illnesses of their birth parents. Your child has the benefit of the healthy environment of your home, where you can influence his behavior to a great degree. Qualified mental health professionals can provide assistance to you and your child and help you work on any danger signs created in the birth family.

CHAPTER 15

Answering the Hard Questions

Your child, as soon as he can talk, will begin to ask you all sorts of questions that pertain to his adoption. Some of these questions may make you uncomfortable. The fact he's adopted is a significant part of his heritage and, therefore, is a reality for you, your child, and the rest of the family. Answering his questions, though they may be tough, will help him understand the reality of his family and the things that happened before he became part of your family.

Strategies for Approaching Questions

Parents who've raised a variety of adopted children say that there are two basic rules to follow when answering your child's questions about adoption. First, use truth and honesty; and second, rely on patience and love. Almost every problem can be addressed with one of these rules. Problems must be faced head on and never brushed aside, no matter how small the question seems or how busy you might feel. Be totally honest, no matter how uncomfortable you may be.

Why Don't I Look Like You?

This question will pop up, especially if you've adopted internationally or outside your ethnic group. At first, your child may point out your difference in color, or perhaps wonder about other differences like height, body type, and facial features.

Celebrating Differences and Similarities

Your explanation will depend on your child's age. Tell your child that nobody looks exactly like anyone else, even twins. You might show him a comparison between your skin color and that of your spouse, which is unlikely to be exactly the same. According to your spiritual philosophy, you might explain that God likes variety and the whole world is full of different skin colors, body shapes, and so on. "God made you, and you look just like he wanted you to."

Alert!

A child may ask the same question over and over. Never resist answering her, and be careful about your tone of voice. Even very small children can pick up on irritation, anxiety, or impatience. It can take lots of repetition for a child to understand and internalize the answers to these tough questions. Consistent answers will help her feel secure in what you are saying.

Too many differences will distance him from you, however, so while you say, "You have a great tan all the time. Your skin is so pretty," also point out how you both love cross-country skiing and can't stand peas. Being a family is about much more than looks, and you can make that point clear.

Jenny, the mom of an adopted biracial child and two biological children, recommends that when your child begins to ask about differences, you dwell on what makes everybody in the family the same. She suggests that you take a basket and put granny smith apples, red delicious apples, and Fuji apples in it and ask your child what is in the basket. He will say "apples," not "red apples, green apples, and yellow apples." Use this logic with things such as nose, ears, eyes, and hair—noses are noses no matter what shape or color. As your child grows older and asks more complex questions, fill in the blanks with more in-depth answers suitable for his age.

Answering Spoken and Unspoken Questions

You will need to answer the underlying assumption in these hard questions as well as the actual verbalized questions. "Why don't I look like you?" is really another way of asking, "Am I really your child?" or "Are we family?"

Not being born to you can make your child anxious. Certain trite adoption statements can increase anxiety; for example, if you say, "We picked you out of all the children," your child may feel like he has to meet a higher standard to deserve being chosen. Acknowledge any anxiety that comes up, and reassure him that you expect him to do his best, but you know nobody's perfect, including yourself. When you make a mistake, show your child how adults admit when they're wrong and say, "I'm sorry," even when the mistake was an accident.

Who Are My Real Parents?

This question usually follows or is asked in place of "Why don't I look like you?" Answer questions about "real" parents as honestly as you can, in a way that doesn't create more questions. Say something like, "Your mother was very young when she got pregnant with you. She had no money, no home, and her boyfriend had left her. She was scared of what was going to happen to her, and what kind of life she was going to provide you with. She decided that the best thing she could do for you was to find a family that would give you all she wanted to but couldn't."

Talk about the Adoption

Don't keep the adoption a big secret from your child, thinking you'll tell her when you think she's old enough. Her adoption is an integral part of who she is, and that adoption changed your whole family's culture, too. She has the right to know about it and have it explained to her as part of her life story.

She should hear the word "adoption" from the time she's an infant. Talk about adoption in the natural course of conversation, but avoid using the word "adopted" when you refer to her, especially when introducing her; "my daughter" is all you need to say. Never say "adopted" when you wouldn't use the term "biological" in conjunction with her status.

Discovering Biological Relationships

"Why couldn't I come from your tummy?" is also a related question. As your child begins to understand how babies grow and notices pregnant women, she will begin to consider why she didn't join your family in the usual way. Talk about how she grew in another woman's tummy. If you have biological children, especially if you get pregnant after you adopt, this question will take on more urgency. You can reinforce that your daughter inherited beautiful curly hair from her biological mother, so she had to come from her, since you wouldn't have been able to give her those curls.

Alert!

If a big part of the relinquishment was due to a birth parent drug or alcohol problem, gloss over the negative things when he is young. Don't lie and say the birth mom was an honor student who never got into trouble, but try to be as neutral as possible.

You want your child to realize that she came from and was (or is) loved by her birth family, but that she's a forever part of your family, and you love her unconditionally. To do this you could post "The

Adoption Creed," a poem by Fleur Conkling Heyliger, in your child's bedroom and or the front entry where everyone can see it:

No flesh of my flesh
Nor bone of my bone
But still miraculously my own
Never forget
For one minute
You grew not under my heart
But in it.

Distinctions between biological and adopted children in your family should be minimal—especially in the way you relate to them. Positive experiences, choices, and connecting over time build families.

You're Not My Real Mom

When your beloved child hurls those words at you, take a deep breath and say, "What does a 'real' mom do?" Turning the statement back on her engages the less emotional part of her brain. Angry feelings precipitated the insult, as well as an emerging sense of independence that all children have.

 Essential

One adoptive mom said she responds with things like, "Is Shadow our real dog?" or "Are those pants your real pants?" when her child says she is not her real mom. You could say, "You hurt my feelings when you say I'm not your real mom (or dad) because I know how much I love you. You are my real child and nothing can change that!"

Explain that real moms and dads:

- Take care of their children
- Give them food, shelter, clean clothes, and love
- Teach them right from wrong
- Guard them from danger
- Encourage and support them
- Love them unconditionally

If you're getting this comment frequently, it indicates an underlying insecurity. One way to deal with this is to make a poster with your child that lists what "real" parents do. Tack the poster to the wall or, better yet, frame it. Post it where your child and everybody else in the family will see it several times a day.

Marti, an adoptive mom in Oregon, adopted her daughter Heidi at age twelve. In addition to the fact that Heidi couldn't understand why her birth parents wouldn't raise her, she'd been in five different foster homes. Because she had been hurt and moved around so much, she continually acted out to see if her parents would really keep her. During her many fits, she'd scream and yell, "You're not my real mom!"

Marti would always say to her, "No, I'm not your real mom, but I'm really your mom."

One day, they were in their church's parking lot and a car almost hit Heidi. Luckily, Marti saw it, yelled, and grabbed Heidi out of the way. Heidi said, "Mom, you saved me!"

And Marti replied, "Honey, I may not be your real mom, but I am really your mom. It's my job to be here and protect you." Marti says she never heard, "You're not my real mom" again.

Recognize your right to parent your child. No matter how much sympathy you may feel for the birth family losing a part of their family, or how unsure you might be about your right to your child, keep in mind that a court made your adoption binding, and nothing anyone says or does will negate it. Adoption is forever, unless you purposefully go back to court and reverse it.

If I'm Really Bad, Will You Give Me Back?

This question usually comes up when your child realizes the difference between adoptive and biological parents. If your child is older and adopted from an institution or endured multiple placements or a failed adoption, you're more likely to hear this question. You may be shocked to hear your child sob, "Are you going to send me back?" after being reprimanded for something simple like scattering toys, teasing his brother, or kicking over the dog's water dish.

Guilt

Children from abusive, neglectful backgrounds usually internalize the abuse and believe that they somehow provoked their parents and deserved the abuse or neglect. "I cried too much" or " I was a bad kid" are common justifications children come to believe.

Other reactions to fear of rejection can be an "I don't care" attitude or outright defiance and rebellion. "I don't care" comes from the protective strategy of shutting down, thus sealing off emotions to numb the pain. Defiance and rebellion come from thinking that says, "I'll reject you before you can reject me."

 Essential

Adopted children often endure tremendous amounts of guilt. Guilt is a terrible weight for a child to carry; when you answer questions quickly and truthfully, the guilty episodes will gradually disappear. Absolving guilt gives your child more room to absorb the real freedom, structure, and boundless love available within your family. Help him to enjoy the feeling that he has the right to be happy.

Magical Thinking

Until they reach the emotional ages of ten or eleven, children tend to believe in wishful or magical thinking. Children who have been moved from their homes or into and out of several foster homes may have this belief reinforced. For example, if your child was frequently afraid in his biological home and wished desperately to escape, then was taken and placed in a foster home, he will think his wish became reality. He may think that the wish made the removal happen, and may believe that any wish he makes can then come true.

Help your child understand that magical thinking doesn't work. Wish out loud for a new car, a new couch, or that your ugly kitchen floor would disappear. Do so several times in the presence of your child. Then ask your child to wish for something specific, like a new video game or pair of shoes. Have him wish with all his might; join him in wishing for a specific item. Discuss that no matter how hard you wish, you really can't make something happen just by wishing or thinking.

Strategies for Reassuring Your Child

You have two main challenges for children who think they're somehow responsible for their adoption or any mistreatment that might have occurred. First, you must establish yourself as the safe, loving adult who's in charge. Second, as discussed in Chapter 14, you must create secure attachment to your child that will allow his personality to unfold.

Attachment to you will allow your child to trust you and trust others as he grows. Attachment issues, depending on the age your child was when you adopted him and his previous circumstances, require a combination of high-energy nurturing and much more structure than normal parenting. High-energy nurturing means you must expend consistent, constant emotional energy over months and even years. High-structure parenting involves clear, workable boundaries that you're committed to establish and maintain. This type of parenting may be viewed by others as too controlling, so be sure you have the help of a support group that understands just what you face. See Chapters 14 and 16 for more detailed discussions about building attachment.

 *Question?*

How can I demonstrate to my child that expressing angry feelings isn't dangerous?
Your child may believe that expressing her fears about an abusive person in her past will make that person suddenly appear. Model that it is okay to talk about anger. You can say, "I'm furious that person hurt you" or "I'm so mad about that person not keeping you safe." Encourage her to express her feelings and show her that expressing them won't make that person reappear.

Why Didn't My Mom Want Me?

Abandonment is any child's greatest fear, and this question is fundamental to your child's self-image. Being relinquished, abandoned, or taken out of the custody of toxic parents are often mixed together in a child's mind. It's hard for a child to determine what really happened and why. Unless you can provide real answers, your child will be unable to move past the trauma to securely attach to your family. You must figure out how to answer her questions without complicating the situation.

Provide Age-Appropriate Explanations

First of all, it is important to reassure your child that, of course her birth mother wanted her. Children must understand that they are wanted. Imagine how it would feel to believe that the person who created you had no feelings for you. You don't want your child to feel this way. When you answer this question, offer details that your child can understand and accept at her age. For example, teenage pregnancy might be a big concept for a four-year-old, but a twelve-year-old is mature enough to understand.

Reinforce the Rightness of Your Adoption

An anonymous writer wrote "Legacy of an Adopted Child" to explain the complexities of adoptive relationships. This might help your child understand the situation as she grows older.

> *Once there were two women who never knew each other. One you do not remember; the other you call Mother.*
>
> *Two different lives, shaped to make your one. One became your guiding star; the other became your sun. The first gave you life; the second taught you how to live in it.*
>
> *The first gave you a need for love; the second was there to give it. One gave you a nationality; the other gave you a name. One gave you the seed of talent; the other gave you an aim. One gave you emotions; the other calmed your fears. One saw your first sweet smile; the other dried your tears.*
>
> *One gave you up—it was all that she could do. The other prayed for a child, and God led her straight to you.*

Will I Have Problems Just Like My Birth Mom Did?

When your child learns negative facts about his birth parents, he may refuse to believe the information or aggressively defend the birth parents. He may become obsessed by the fear that he'll end up the same way. He may worry that inherited traits will mean he has no control over where he ends up in life.

Help him understand that he has much more control than he thinks. Also, figure out why he's worried. He may have seen something on television or heard remarks in school that reinforce statements such as "Like father, like son" or "She's a chip off the old block."

Understanding Choices Versus Illness

Explain the fact that a predisposition for a particular illness or disorder doesn't mean your child will suffer the same one his birth parent did. Some things have genetic links and others don't. Even if something has a genetic link, it does not mean your child will necessarily carry that gene. Emphasize that you will love and care for your child no matter what happens to him.

Make sure your child understands the difference between personal choices and illnesses or disorders. Negative choices, as in drug or alcohol addictions, burglary, or assault, are within the control of individuals and are by no means genetic.

Alert!

Always express any displeasure for your child's behavior in a firm but loving way. Avoid using physical or shaming punishments, neither of which are really appropriate parenting techniques, especially for children from abusive backgrounds.

While a predisposition for addiction can be genetic, it does not mean your child will be an addict. In fact, addiction is a self-inflicted disease—abusing drugs or alcohol starts the process. Certain behavior may put your child at risk of repeating his birth parent's addiction, but you, his parent, can help him avoid the risk. If he doesn't start using drugs or alcohol, he doesn't need to worry about succumbing to the same problem.

Don't Compete with the Birth Family

While you have to be realistic, avoid the temptation to point out how much better your home is than the one your child came from. Don't make any direct comparisons, because his self-esteem will force him to defend that home. Focus on the positive things in your family without making comparisons. Say, "Doesn't it feel good to snuggle into clean sheets and soft blankets?" as you tuck him in at night.

Did You Adopt Me Because You Couldn't Have Your Own Kids?

Implicit in this question is the same underlying thought as "Why don't I look like you?" If you experienced infertility, the pain of that memory can complicate your answer. Be sure you've resolved your own issues about never having given birth. Even very young children can pick up on the remarks and attitudes of adults. It's important to stress that first of all, the adopted child is your own child, and that we all experience difficult times in our lives. Emphasize how very thrilled you are to be her parent and say that you don't regret a single moment of the life journey that brought you to her.

If you adopted a child, then found yourself pregnant, people who've known about your infertility may say, "Isn't it wonderful you're finally having your own baby?" Especially if this dumb statement is made in front of your child, firmly say, "We're all so happy to be having our second child."

Addressing the Underlying Issue

Never make any comments or behave as if adopting were a less desirable choice. It's a different choice, one that not everybody may be able to make. It takes people who have self-confidence, emotional strength, and an ability to love unconditionally.

If you get pregnant after adopting, be careful to deflect an overabundance of showers and gifts that your friends and extended family may bestow upon you and your biological child. Speak directly to your parents and in-laws (who may be thrilled you're finally producing a "blood" grandchild). Insist that no distinction be made between the new baby and your daughter. When family heirlooms are discussed, be sure that all your children receive the same consideration. Don't accept one child receiving more than another.

The Hard Questions Can Be Answered

You will build attachment bonds with your child as you lovingly and appropriately address his questions and the emotions that underlie those questions. Explain biological connections in a way that underscores the importance of choice and environment. Reassure your child that he has power over how his life progresses, that he is safe to love and thrive in your family.

Maintaining Biological and Adoptive Connections
Ideally, your child will have the assurance of being part of your family forever, while knowing about his biological connections. He should be attached to you, but have bonds with safe members of his birth family when possible. Those bonds will give him an understanding that he came from some place concrete.

Adoption identity issues can become complicated by the identity issues that normally surface during adolescence. If you have an adolescent, follow these rules:

- Don't take behavior personally
- Stay calm
- Be consistent
- Set reasonable boundaries
- Award appropriate consequences

These points will help you maintain your sanity during what is probably the most trying period of your child's life.

CHAPTER 16

Creating and Strengthening Family Bonds

The adoptive family has bonds like any other family. Depending on when and how your child joined your family, you may find that you need to consciously work at growing and supporting your family bonds. The stronger the bonds you all develop to each other, the healthier your family will be.

Prepare to Build Bonds

The more you prepare before your child joins the family, the more smoothly the whole process will proceed and the easier it will be to create and strengthen your bonds with your child. Your preparation should include you and your extended family. You need to understand what kind of situation your child is coming from. You also must be aware of your own strengths and weaknesses, especially your ability to respond positively to negative situations and avoid losing your temper.

Understand Your Child's Reality
As you plan to form a family with a new child, it is important to get as much information as possible about the life your child had before you. Even if you are adopting an infant, prenatal information is important because it can have an impact on how your child bonds.

Alert!

A study in *Psychiatry News* showed that children of parents who are highly stressed are more likely to become ill, particularly with fevers, than other children. Reducing the stress in your home will go a long way toward creating a safe, healthy, and comforting environment for your child. Keep in mind, though, that all parents experience some stress and you can only do your best for your situation.

The older your child is at the time of his adoption, the greater your challenges will be, with the exception that a teenager who wants to be adopted may give you fewer problems than a younger child with limited verbal skills. Teenagers have the cognitive abilities to know the importance of a family, and they must agree to being adopted or remain in foster care. Since they can make the choice and are not forced into anything, they are much more likely to be cooperative and participate in figuring out what needs to be done to attach to you and your family.

Understand Your Strengths and Weaknesses

You and your spouse (or the person who will be your main support) should assess, in writing, your strengths and weaknesses as a family. Children already in your home should also do this exercise. List four to six strengths and weaknesses independently.

For example, your strengths might include:

- We talk over concerns rather than keeping them to ourselves.
- We eat a meal together every day.
- We have sufficient financial resources to provide the necessities and some of the luxuries of life.
- We stick up for each other and don't let other people put any of our members down.

Examples of weaknesses might include:

- We don't have a regular bedtime.
- Our vehicles are old and unreliable.
- We have conflicting ideas about and methods of discipline.
- One of us is passive and the other aggressive.

After you have listed your strengths and weaknesses, get together and compare your notes. Make a master list of the strengths that you agree on and post it in a prominent place. This statement of strengths will help you focus when the inevitable challenges come. It will also help you be realistic about the challenges you are equipped to handle.

 Essential

> Donna, a single mom of two daughters adopted from Hungary, said, "Before I brought Tanya and Lissa home, I made a poster about why I would be a good mom. My social worker helped me write it, and I can't tell you how many times I felt like giving up and didn't, because I could see right there in front of me why I was a good mom."

Set aside time to discuss the weaknesses, one at a time, and how you will eliminate them, improve on them, or turn them into strengths. Don't rush through this process. All parents interviewed for this book who avoided or were able to work through serious issues emphasized the importance of being realistic about how their families functioned.

Prepare Your Relatives for Bonding

Just as adoption requires the building of bonds in your immediate family, your extended family will need to bond with your child as well. Your mother, siblings, or whoever lives near enough to be there for you can help you show your child how a functional family comes together for mutual benefit and will come to develop loving bonds with your child.

You and your child will need the support and care your parents, grandparents, and siblings can offer when problems emerge. The reaction of extended family members to your child's testing of boundaries can make your job easier if handled appropriately. The development of a bonded relationship between your child and a relative is similar to the process your child will go through with you. It takes time and shared experiences to build bonds.

Encourage your child to spend time with and develop relationships with grandparents, cousins, and aunts. Memories created with extended family who primarily offer love and affection (without the added responsibilities of day-to-day parenting) can be some of the most cherished from childhood. If you have adopted an older child, you need to give everyone involved the time and space to get to know and love each other.

Understanding a Relative's Perspective

You may have been caught up in the excitement of adoption and may not really know how your relatives feel. Your parents, grandparents, and siblings may be worried about possible heartbreak for you, should something go wrong with the adoption. If they don't have any experience with adoption or adopted children, they may wonder whether or not your child is really going to be part of the family.

For example, when Jeanne and her husband decided to adopt their third child, Jeanne was worried about telling her mother they wanted to adopt an African American toddler. Jeanne's mother told her that the idea of adoption itself worried her, not the race of the child. She was concerned that she'd never love an adopted grandchild like her own flesh and blood. But when Jeanne's mother attended the placement ceremony and heard the readings and watched her daughter, son-in-law, and their children with the toddler, Matt, she knew it was right. When the judge placed Matt in Jeanne's arms as a symbol of her responsibility and commitment to him, her mom said she felt just as she had when she came to the birth rooms and saw her newborn grandchildren. That child was her grandchild and she loved him, immediately.

Sitting down and having conversations, probably more than one, will clear up any misconceptions and bring you critical assistance. It will also clear the way for your family to feel ready to develop a bond with your child.

Teaching What Family Is

All children, adopted or not, need to understand the importance of family. Helping your child see that family is the backbone of her life is an important lesson. Children who have developmental delays may not be able to immediately or completely understand how a family is different from institutions or other social organizations. The love, acceptance, and support that typifies a normal family may seem odd or unfamiliar to these children. They may be used to the "every man for himself" standard of behavior. If they had caregivers that rotated through their lives, they may not have become attached to anyone in particular, and they may have internalized that they could only depend on themselves.

 *Question?*

How do I answer those who pity me for "having to" adopt?
Tell them your family formed by adoption isn't second best to those formed by birth, and in significant ways it may be superior. Explain that there are many studies that show adoptive families surpass the general population in positive outcomes for their children. Offer that adoption has been a wonderful experience and you recommend it for everyone.

You can help your child understand family by using concrete symbols. Draw a picture of your family together and label each person. You could draw a house or a heart around the entire family and explain that you all belong to each other and share a home and a life. Use dolls or stuffed animals to show your child how parents care for children. You can also practice visualization with your child. Ask her to close her eyes and imagine you, her, and the other members of your immediate family all standing in a circle with your arms around each other, smiling. Giving her a physical image of family bonds can encourage her to form them.

Integrating Adopted Children into the Family

Depending on your child's age, you can use a variety of methods to claim him and help him feel connected to you and the rest of your family. Refer to the description of the stages of attachment in Chapter 13 and figure out which stage your child is in.

Start with his specific stage and work backward, if necessary, adapting specific techniques for his developmental age. In addition to these methods, it is important to take time at the beginning of your family's adoption journey to allow bonds to develop.

Cocooning

In addition to rituals such as claiming and naming your child, another claiming technique that is recommended by adoption experts is cocooning when your child is first placed with you. Cocooning refers to pulling away a bit from the outside world and focusing your time and attention on your immediate family. This allows you to build bonds that will lead to secure attachment. How you cocoon will depend on your child's age and your family's needs. You could, for example, plan to stay home together for an entire week without answering the phone or turning on the TV. You could declare that each night after six is family time and is a time for games, stories, and sharing. You could take a month and avoid any social outings, instead taking the time to just be a family together. If you've adopted an infant, you will want to spend a lot of time just holding him. If you have adopted an older child who is more self-sufficient than an infant, he may not be interested in being physically held for long periods of time. However, he will benefit greatly by you giving just as much undivided attention to him as you would an infant.

 Essential

Delores and Tim wanted to adopt sisters. They held a family council with their children—three girls and a boy. The three girls were enthusiastic, but the boy sat mutely. Finally, Tim managed to get him to blurt out, "There's too many girls in this family, already!" He wanted a brother, not more sisters. Eventually, they adopted two boys. Be sure that the decision to add more children to the family through adoption is supported by the entire family.

When you cocoon, you may need to explain to those outside your immediate family, that you will welcome visits in a few weeks, but right now you're going to concentrate on your child. Ask your extended family for help in this process if necessary. Grandma or grandpa, uncles and aunts can run errands, do grocery shopping, help with housework, and in other ways give you the time and space to learn about your child. Even though you didn't go through pregnancy and birth, you, your partner, and your child need the bonding time most families take when a baby is born to them.

Have Fun Together as a Family

Other than meeting basic needs of care and survival, giggling and enjoying each other's company is the single best way to build secure attachment. Enjoy games, cartoons, and funny stories with your child. Laughter, smiles, and other positive emotions release feel-good chemicals into your child's brain and into yours.

Be open to seeing the silly or humorous side of mistakes or mishaps. You will be modeling appropriate responses to unfortunate happenings that were either accidents or unavoidable. An older child whose early experiences with adults may have involved anger, will learn to trust you much more quickly if you can laugh at yourself and see the funny side of things. Keep one caveat in mind, however—never laugh at your child, only with him, and avoid sarcasm or teasing at all costs.

Shared Experiences Are Key

You can joke around with your children and cocoon for the first few weeks, but if you don't take the time to be a family through all the stages of your child's life, you will not develop close bonds. It is one thing to know you are part of a family, but it is another to experience it on a daily basis. Yes, you as a parent may have a job, friends, activities, hobbies, and responsibilities, but your family must be one of the primary focuses of your life for your child to really experience family life.

This doesn't mean you must spend the rest of your life saying, "Okay, today we're going to focus on our family togetherness, everyone!" It does mean that you stay involved in your child's life, keep him involved in yours, and create a wide variety of ways in which you regularly interact with each other and share things.

Set Up a Chosen Day and Other Strategies

Establishing traditions specific to your adoption are critical in helping your child feel bonded to your family. Just what those traditions are should be dictated by your particular circumstances—the placement age of your child, your status as a single or partnered parent, and attitudes of your extended family members. Consider setting aside a specific day each year to celebrate when your child first entered your home, the adoption was finalized, or other occasion unique to your child. Families call this day Chosen Day, Gotcha Day, Our Special Day, The Placement Ceremony, or other descriptive names. This is a special day like a birthday, but it's more significant. A birthday is a day to celebrate the child; this kind of day is a day to celebrate your bond together.

Examples of Chosen or Placement Day Activities

Your agency may host the initial placement ceremony, when you can take pictures and memorialize the event. You may want to write up something that describes your feelings that can be preserved in your child's life book or memory box. Some families sing hymns or songs or read scriptures.

After the actual ceremony, it's often nice to have refreshments or go to lunch or dinner as a group. Some families host an open house or friends do the honors. There are no hard and fast rules—just do what feels right to you and your family. Your child may get it mixed up with her birthday when she's younger, but that's okay. Two birthdays are something to be treasured!

Older children should be involved in planning the placement ceremony or celebration. Let them pick out the food, make up the guest list, and help prepare the invitations. The guest list should include all of her new family members, as well as teachers, social workers, foster parents, birth family members (if appropriate and within the adoption guidelines), therapists or others she wants to witness the event.

 Essential

One family described setting up a table with a unity candle. Their new son lit one candle and the mom and dad lit another during the ceremony. Then the parents, the two siblings, and the son used their candles to light the center candle together to signify the joining of their lives.

If you give your child gifts on this day, consider gifts that reflect you and your family. Find things that you can use to express a reminder of your permanent commitment.

Strengthening Your Family's Primary Relationship

Your family is built on the relationship between you and your spouse or partner. If you are going to take on the challenges of children, then it is necessary to be humble enough to get help when you need it. Reach out to your spouse or partner; talk regularly, or pray or meditate together, and set aside couple time.

Many people wrongly believe that adding children to a family will help heal problems in the marriage; in fact, the opposite is true. If you have any marital problems, the challenge of being parents can bring them to the forefront. As you parent, you must learn to be patient with each other and accepting of your differing parenting styles. You might not do things the same way, but if you both do things in a way that brings about the same result (a safe, loving home), then the method should not be as important as the outcome.

Use Support to Strengthen Your Relationship

Build an extended network to give you the support you must have, a network of family and friends who approve and validate your adoption and give you the support you need to maintain a healthy marriage or relationship with your partner. For example, many parents find their greatest support system through active participation in a religious community.

In addition, seek professional counseling when necessary. Having wise counsel available isn't just an adoption issue, it's a parenting and marriage issue. Find a professional who will help you through the postadoption process.

Read and listen to information that pertains to your family's issues on a regular basis. Subscribe to adoption magazines and newsletters, both online and in print. Keep a private journal to help you understand your feelings, your relationship, and how your behavior affects your child's behavior. Note that an online blog can be a useful tool, but it can't take the place of a private journal—blogs are too public and you should be cautious about revealing your innermost concerns and feelings or details about your child's life online.

 *Question?*

> **How can I find an adoption professional who meets my family's needs?**
> Talk to other adoptive parents whose children have similar backgrounds to yours. Also, ask your agency for a referral. Then ask for a preliminary interview. Be sure you understand the person and feel he understands you. In addition, assess whether the person is knowledgeable about adoption issues or is willing to put you in contact with those who are.

Enhancing Sibling Bonds

Sibling bonds within your family will give your child perspective and a sense of security. Sibling bonds are almost as important as attachments with parents. Helping your child maintain healthy relationships with siblings will ensure he feels connected. Every parent wants smiling, loving children who are one another's best friends, but that goal can seem very far away when they're screaming at each other over who used up the shampoo or punching each other and yelling, "I called the front" in a race to the car.

Consistently reinforce "We're a family" and "We're a team." If you adopt a younger child, prepare the older one ahead of time. Role play what it will be like when the baby comes home. Many parents recommend that you give your older child a doll that he can practice diapering and holding.

 *Alert!*

Acknowledge an older sibling's feelings when a baby comes into the family. Tell her about things people said when she was a baby. Remember some of the gifts or cards she was given. Get out photos from when she entered your family and help her understand her arrival was just as special.

Parents who adopt internationally advise taking the older child to pick up the younger. Also, if you don't have a partner and spouse to make it a family trip, enlist Grandma, an uncle, or a good friend, because dividing your attention will be impossible. Generally, the older child will adapt more readily to the new sibling if he is allowed to be there right from the start, rather than being left behind.

However, make the decision carefully—consider all aspects of your trip and your child's personality, especially if you're picking up your new child from an orphanage in a poverty-stricken country; the experience may be too intense for some children. See Chapter 13 for more about sibling bonds.

Sibling Rivalry

If your adopted child comes into a family that already contains children, you must help him feel part of the group. If he's an infant or toddler, the process should be relatively easy, because everybody responds to babies. However, if he replaces someone as the baby of the family, then you'll deal with sibling rivalry, just as in birth families. If you adopt a child that is preschool or elementary aged and you already have children in this age range, sibling rivalry is also likely.

Sibling rivalry is normal, but you can mitigate it in various ways. Ensure that your current children don't feel pushed aside by the newcomer. They should be secure in their attachment to you, and they should trust that you will continue to meet their needs for nurturing and structure. You can demonstrate your love for them through your consistency in meeting needs, establishing reasonable boundaries, and awarding appropriate consequences when family rules and boundaries are broken. When adopting or having additional children after your first adopted child, carefully consider how ready your first adopted child really is for a sibling. Your child may have developed a certain level of self-sufficiency, but might not have formed a secure attachment with you. Introducing another child, whether by adoption or biologically, can intensify attachment weaknesses, leading to sibling rivalry and other problematic behaviors.

 *Fact*

Linda Sonna's book, *The Everything® Parent's Guide to Raising Siblings*, contains excellent advice on controlling competition and rivalry and settling squabbles. She also addresses the issue of adopted siblings and preparing your biological children for the placement, as well as what to do about helping to forge bonds.

Your adopted child may wrongly believe the other children are somehow more real members of the family than he is. Make it clear to everyone that there is no priority among children, that you love all of them, and that each has his or her own important place in the family. It is also important to allow all members of the family to express their feelings and work through anger and jealousy in safe ways.

Coping with Changing Sibling Roles

If you had an only child when you decided to adopt, you will deal with issues of learning to share space, attention, and your love. If your firstborn child gains an older sibling, your problems will multiply exponentially. Birth order is extremely important to all children, and giving up the very real first place can be traumatic. Many adoption experts will caution you about disrupting the birth order in your family. If you have a relative who needs a kinship placement of a child older than your own and you feel that your obligations to your extended family member outweigh any discomfort your current child might have, be sure to engage the services of a reliable and competent therapist who understands adoption issues and can help your child work through problems.

Strengthening Sibling Bonds

One of the hardest lessons to learn as a parent is that your children will have their own independent relationship with each other that has little to do with you. You can teach them to treat each other with love and respect, but at some point, you have to step back and let them create their own relationship. This doesn't mean you have to let a war break out. There are things you can do to help them strengthen their bond and appreciate each other, so that as they grow into adults they will have a strong bond to rely on.

Help your kids understand what there is to appreciate about each other. Point out the unique and wonderful qualities they each have and find ways this can be meaningful to them: "Look, Damian, Amanda's outside shooting baskets. You're so good at that, I'll bet she would love it if you gave her some pointers."

Allow them to create shared experiences. Sometimes as a parent you just have to remove yourself from the situation. Let them play with modeling clay alone together, or go into the next room while they're playing checkers together. They need space to relate to each other in their own way. Being nearby is fine, but you should not try to micromanage them.

Help them see that disagreements are not fatal. Siblings argue all of the time, whether they are biological or adopted. It's not the end of the world if they get mad at each other or disagree. Help them work through it and get to the other side. Sometimes, it is helpful to not get involved at all and see if they can work it out on their own.

CHAPTER 17

Unique Discipline Issues for Adopted Children

Your adopted child is likely to experience the normal ups and downs of childhood. However, some adopted children may experience unusual behavior problems that can make discipline a challenge. This is most likely to occur if you adopt an older child who experienced an abusive situation or was extremely neglected, either in a home or an institution. You will love your child no matter what kind of behavior he exhibits, but it is a good idea to understand some of the possibilities that children in these unique situations may face and consider the best ways to handle them.

Hurtful Statements

There may come a time when your child will try to use words to hurt you or punish you. "You're not my real dad," "You don't really love me," "I hate you," or "You just adopted me to get someone to do work around the house" are the kinds of statements or accusations your child might yell at you. Remember that the actual words your child is saying are not what are important. You both know those kinds of statements aren't true, so it doesn't make sense to spend a lot of time answering them directly. Your child may be lashing out at you because she's feeling insecure and wants you to reaffirm your forever commitment. This is especially true for children who've been abandoned or who have come through the foster care system.

Alert!

Be aware that all children, adopted or biological, may say things they don't mean when angry. "I wish I'd never been born" or "I wish you were never my mother" are words teens can hurl at their parents when they're disappointed or upset at being told no.

A child who uses hurtful words may be trying to exert control, to manipulate you and your emotions. She's probably well aware that her words sting. You should calmly ask why she wants to hurt you by saying something so untrue. You may be surprised by her answer when you address this in such a direct manner. She may blink and say she's sorry or she may reveal a deep fear of being sent back to the orphanage, removed from the home, or rejected if she's bad enough.

When your child says something hurtful to you, stay calm and turn the statement or question back to her. By doing so, you model appropriate responses to words that are upsetting, show that it is not appropriate to react with anger, and demonstrate that it is important to try to understand why the words were spoken. Finally, don't get into a fight—something emotionally fragile children may try to push their parents into.

Understanding Your Child's Reality

If you adopt an older child, it means that you have to accept that a piece of her heart will remain somewhere else. What she experienced and who was responsible may be locked inside and only come out when she is finally secure enough to remember. Your efforts to get your child to attach to you may allow her to feel safe in saying hurtful things. You must be strong enough to recognize her internal conflicts. This is especially true if you've adopted a child from an institution or foster care, or if your child has emotional disabilities.

Maintain Consistency and Avoid Anger

Most children know just which buttons to push in order to create emotional upset in their parents, and they may seem to get real pleasure from the process. This is especially true of children who were neglected or abused before adoption. In fact, adoption researchers have concluded that adopted children provoke their parents to anger as a form of control and manipulation that comes from feeling helpless.

As a parent, you need to learn to control your own temper and always be conscious of the fact that your behavior provides a role model for your child. If you acknowledge that your child's sadness, fear, and anger underlies his behavior and react calmly and lovingly, you will strengthen his attachment to you. His attachment will allow him to learn better behavior.

 *Fact*

> Dr. Karyn Purvis's book, *The Connected Child*, gives an in-depth discussion of strategies that have worked for families who have adopted preschool- or elementary-aged children from abusive backgrounds. She demonstrates how ordinary discipline techniques often fail for unattached, traumatized, or emotionally fragile children.

Recognizing Your Role in Problems

It takes two to tango, and sometimes when a child misbehaves or acts out, the parent has played a role in bringing that behavior to light. That is not to say that you are the cause of your child's problems. However, parents can unintentionally do things that actually ratchet situations up a level. For example, did you push through your preschooler's normal naptime to get some errands done and then he had a meltdown in the middle of the grocery store? No one is perfect, and there may be times when your child's behavior is impacted by the fact that you didn't notice something that was going on or did not respond to it appropriately. It can also be easy to react to your child's behavior with anger, adding fuel to the fire.

You and Your Spouse or Partner Should Agree

Before your child comes home to you, discuss parenting styles and discipline strategies with your spouse or partner. Commit to each other that you will work out any misunderstandings or differences behind closed doors and not in front of your child. You must always present a united front, because your child must know that he can't divide and conquer, something most children attempt at least a few times.

If you adopt a baby, you'll have some time to work out compromises and strategies, but if you adopt a toddler or older child, you must know from day one how your partner will react.

Understand that neither of you can read the other's mind, and what you think is important may not be important to your partner. If you're a single parent, you must still line up a support person who will align himself with you and agree with the kind of parenting required by your situation.

Stay in Charge and Set an Example

If your adopted child has behavior issues that put other children in the family or school setting at risk, you have an obligation to protect them. You may have to physically remove your child from the setting, and you must take control. How you do so, however, will be critical.

The following are some strategies for disciplining children who are unable to respond normally:

- **Clarify expectations and offer simple choices.** For example, say, "Use your words. You may not kick your sister. Tell her you are angry, then either sit in your mad chair or ask me to help you make a better choice."

- **Respond quickly and present consequences.** Your child's emotional centers drove him to lash out and he may not remember hitting or pinching after a few minutes. This is why you or your support person must be close enough to intercede and why you must always award an appropriate consequence.
- **Retrain and redo.** Simple punishment doesn't work for some children. Stop the behavior, then help your child go back to the point where he made the wrong choice, and guide him to a better choice.
- **Offer praise for success.** Just as you can't ignore negative behavior, you must reinforce good behavior, over and over again.

In taking control, you must be careful not to yell or even speak loudly; your actions should be calm and immediate. Again, most of all, you must model how caring adults respond to upsetting situations.

If your child is a significant danger to himself or others, get professional advice. He could need in-patient treatment, but usually you can solve the problem with the help of your support system and a good therapist. A child in this situation has probably been ordered around and manipulated by adults who hurt, belittled, or damaged him.

 Essential

Be sure you understand your child's developmental level when you figure out consequences for misbehavior. For example, if your five-year-old throws a fit at the dinner table, or exhibits some other unacceptable behavior, it's okay to remove him from the scene for a few minutes. Trying to have an in-depth, rational discussion with him about his behavior is not age appropriate and will not be effective.

Fighting

Fighting and acting-out behaviors are counterproductive, but they may be how your child learned to survive in an institution, the streets, or a dysfunctional, abusive home. Your child may have learned to get her needs met through anger and fierce tantrums, or she may have been physically abused and felt completely helpless.

Fighting at School

Fighting at school can be a serious problem, because it means your child hasn't learned how to positively manage disagreements, disappointments, and other negative situations or emotions. Children do not naturally learn how to get along and interact without experiencing varying levels of emotional intensity and conflict; sometimes extreme anger or aggression. The adults in their lives must teach them how to form and manage relationships that work for everyone.

Much concrete teaching about relationships starts when your child becomes verbal. Intervene when your child calls another a bad name or threatens physical harm. Say, "People do not hit each other" and "You may not use those words. Those words are unkind and hurtful."

Help your child learn how to avoid conflict. Teach her how to walk away from an insult and how to turn her attention away from people who make her angry. Offer her tools to use to control anger, such as counting, deep breathing, and using words.

Alert!

Even when you must caution or rebuke a child, always do so in a positive way, and use the "Rule of Three" that many therapists recommend, by offering three positive statements for every negative one.

As your child enters school, teach her about how excluding another child is wrong, and help her develop empathy. Watch for the cliques and groups that can develop. Monitor what is happening with her behavior at school by checking in with teachers or school social workers often. If your child exhibits violence at school, there must be consequences at home for this as well. It's very important that you work in tandem with the school and your child's therapist to deal with school situations.

Dealing with Bullies

Your child may become a target of bullies because of her adopted status, especially if she has issues that make her socially awkward. You must always be on your child's side if she is being excluded or bullied.

Use role playing to give a child who is targeted by a bully specific tools for dealing with the situation. Help your child practice how to walk away from a bully or report bullying behavior to an adult.

Addressing Violence in General

Violence is usually directed toward another person or a person's property. Violence involves both victims and perpetrators. Many perpetrators were victims as young children and gained a sense of control by becoming the stronger one. This may not apply to your child right now, but think about how you would respond if your child becomes either a victim or a bully.

Quarrelling and fighting can lead to violence. Always deal with beginning episodes of violence promptly. Don't be guilty of ignoring behavior until it has become so severe that someone gets hurt. Children who have been abused and or neglected have anger issues. Fear often drives violent behavior, so dealing with the underlying reasons may enable your child to change.

Strategies for de-escalating outbursts include:

- **Distraction:** Try to shift your child's attention
- **Acknowledgment:** Validate the feeling as neutrally as possible
- **Respond:** Provide nurturing comfort, attention, and empathy

Violent tendencies can also have a genetic component, and may be reinforced by early poor parenting. If your child reacts violently or has an emotional illness that causes inappropriate acting out, you can't manage alone—you definitely need extra help from professionals with experience in adoption issues.

Sexual Abuse

It can be upsetting to read about sexual abuse, but it is an unfortunate fact that some children who are adopted from orphanages or the foster care system may have been victims of sexual abuse or witnesses to it. Those who have been abused are at greater risk of becoming offenders themselves as teens or adults, so intervention and therapy is critical.

Being aware of your child's history and knowing what to watch for are powerful tools for preventing or mitigating abuse.

Understanding Sexual Abuse

Sexual abuse ranges from a perpetrator engaging a child in play that involves touching a child's genitals or other private areas and coaxing him to touch his or hers to full penetration. Older children and teens sometimes abuse younger children, especially if they're in a dysfunctional home or institution together. Such children were likely abused themselves as preschoolers or toddlers.

Suspect that your child has been molested in some way if he:

- Has nightmares about things coming at him
- Is withdrawn and anxious
- Uses explicitly sexual behaviors, such as inappropriate touch or gestures to get what he wants

Young children are naturally curious about their bodies and physical differences, but their curiosity is benign, more along the lines of "You show me yours and I'll show you mine" that occurs, under normal circumstances, around age five or six. This is nothing to be concerned about. This age also plays "doctor," but touching or acting out is a sign of problems and should be evaluated by a therapist right away.

Helping Your Child Heal

If you know, suspect, or have evidence that your child has been molested, don't be afraid to touch him in appropriate ways. Part of your parenting role is to help him understand the difference between the hugs, pats, and affection that happen in attached families and the inappropriate touch that was forced on him. A good therapist can help you learn exactly how to approach your child and gradually help him understand good touch.

Like any good parent, you bathe and clean your little children. If your toddler or preschooler has been molested, be very gentle when you bathe or wipe his bottom. Use a spray to clean him after toileting, rather than your hands, until you've established trust. Also, discuss the situation with your pediatrician or therapist.

Alert!

After learning about the sexual abuse of your adopted child, you might be nervous about providing normal care for her. Don't worry; just teach good hygiene by describing what you are doing. For example, "I'm wiping off all the poopie so your bottom doesn't get sore." When your child graduates out of diapers, have her take over the actual washing while you supervise.

You will need all of your emotional strength to deal with a child who has been sexually abused—don't try to do it alone. Your child's spirit and emotions have been devastated, and such wounds heal much more slowly than broken bones or torn muscles.

Dealing with a Child Perpetrator

All too often, helpless victims turn into perpetrators, sometimes as young as eight or nine. When they become physically strong enough to exercise control over younger children, they may begin to act out.

Be concerned if your elementary-aged child sneaks away to be alone with a preschool- or toddler-aged child. Always supervise play and interactions; never leave a newly adopted or foster child alone with a younger child until you are confident about whether or not inappropriate activities will occur.

Also important to supervision is clear, ongoing communication about relationships, trust, and responsibility. If you know, or suspect, that your child has been sexually abused, get him into therapy and don't put him in unsupervised situations where he would have the opportunity to offend.

Eating Disorders and Self-Harm

Eating disorders have become epidemic. There are even Web sites where teens can find out how to hide anorexia (low body weight and body image distortion) or bulimia (overeating and purging or fasting) from their parents. Magazines and videos glamorize extreme thinness.

Scratching, hitting, or cutting oneself has recently become a fad practiced by some adolescents, and it should never be ignored.

Children turn to harming themselves for two main reasons: they're insecure people-pleasers who do not know what to do with their true, unexpressed feelings; or they suffer from psychological pain. Children adopted after infancy are susceptible to both eating disorders and self-harming behaviors, because they may have negative attachment issues.

When to Become Concerned

Signs that your daughter (girls are more likely than boys to have an eating disorder, but don't rule it out for a boy) may have an eating disorder include:

- Exercising excessively
- Eating very little
- Rapid weight loss or gain
- Complaining that she's fat

You may find evidence of laxative or diuretic use. Wearing baggy clothes and refusing to wear T-shirts or shorts can also be significant. Baggy clothing covers up scrawny arms and legs. Be suspicious if the gallon of ice cream you bought a few days ago disappears and nobody will acknowledge eating it—eating disorders often involve secret eating. Also, watch out for a child who insists on going to the bathroom immediately after eating or who takes a shower after eating, since running water masks the sounds of vomiting.

Signs that your child may be a cutter include:

- Bloody tissues, rags, or razors in the garbage
- Wearing baggy clothing or refusal to wear shorts or T-shirts

Arms and legs, especially thighs, are where children cut most frequently. Cutters will hide their behavior by cutting their chests or abdomens, too.

Dealing with Self-Harming Behaviors

Bulimia, anorexia, and self-injurious behavior (SIB) can be treated if they're caught early enough. Your biggest problem may be recognizing the symptoms as soon as they start, because you probably can't quite believe the fact that your child could ignore the pain of hunger or willingly be cutting herself.

A SIB is an addictive behavior that cannot be overcome by willpower. Ultimatums and cajoling will only increase your child's desire to release her inner turmoil through cutting. She will become more ashamed and more isolated, certain that she's worthless and you don't love her. Telling her to stop won't help—she is unable to stop.

If you suspect that your child might be cutting herself, schedule a doctor's appointment with a physician for an examination of arms, legs, chest, and abdomen. Tell the doctor ahead of time what you suspect. If you find evidence, get a referral to a specialist in adolescent self-harm.

 **Fact**

> SIB can include, not only cutting, but also head banging and burning. These behaviors indicate deep underlying issues and sorrows that the person can't express verbally. He cuts, burns, even breaks his own bones to express his pain and relieve the emptiness he feels inside.

If you suspect an eating disorder, see a physician. Your child needs to be weighed and have an examination. Confronting a child with a possible eating disorder will not likely stop the behavior, since it is a way to exhibit control over her own body. Telling her to eat is not going to help—it is important that you work with a therapist who is experienced in eating disorders.

Important Reassurances

Don't let the cautions and descriptions in this chapter scare you, because most adopted children grow up to be happy, productive adults without these kinds of problems.

Violence, sexual predation, and self-harming behaviors happen when children are subjected to abuse and neglect during their most helpless time of life. You, and other adoptive parents, who tackle the difficult task of loving and healing a sad, hurting child do more to change what's wrong with our society than any group, institution, or government agency.

When things get tough, turn to professionals and other support systems, including adoptive parents who are a little further down the road, and your family and friends.

CHAPTER 18

Searching for Your Adopted Child's Birth Family

If you have a completely open adoption, you might think this chapter doesn't pertain to you. However, if your adoption starts out as open but becomes closed because you lose track of the birth family, then you may need to consider searching at some point. Searching for the birth family is a personal situation for each adopted person. Some are afraid to stir up trouble or hurt their adoptive families. Others genuinely have no real inclination beyond curiosity to make contact. Often, certain major events such as divorce, death, or birth trigger a desire to search for one's birth parents.

Thinking Through the Search

Although you and your child may have discussed and planned for years to find his birth parents, those parents may have put the adoption out of their minds and formed a separate life. Your child may have built up fantasies, especially during adolescence, when he chaffed at rules and restrictions. If your son came to you through foster care, contact was probably forbidden until he became an adult.

Perhaps you adopted a child right after birth and your child has always known he was adopted. No matter what the circumstances, a search is a very emotional process and is not something to take lightly.

Coping with Your Own Fears

The search for birth parents is an important emotional journey for your child. You may feel a bit conflicted about the whole search. On the one hand, you want to support your child, on the other hand, you worry about what the results of the search will mean for you.

No matter when you adopted your child, you are his real parents. That connection will not change if you undertake a search. You may be worried that your child will automatically bond more greatly to the birth parents, decide that you aren't an adequate parent, or feel your family was some poor substitute. Rest assured, your child is a part of your family. Finding a birth parent may be an important journey for him, but it does not have to disrupt your bond.

 Fact

A study of American adolescents performed by the Search Institute found that 72 percent of adopted adolescents wanted to know why they were adopted; 65 percent wanted to meet their birth parents; and 94 percent wanted to know which birth parent they looked like.

Understand Birth Parent Emotions

The search for birth parents is not just about your child and his need to know. The search can have a huge impact on the birth parents themselves, so it is important for you and your child to consider what the birth parent went through at the time of the adoption and how he or she may be feeling now.

A birth parent who chooses an open adoption does so in order to have some control over the placement and have the ability to stay in touch. Many open adoptions work out, and the child is never in a position to have to search. Unfortunately, some open adoptions do not work. The adoptive parents might cut off contact, the birth parent might drift away and lose touch, or the birth parent might make a decision to remove herself from the situation. Whatever happens, it's important to remember that the adoption is a very emotional situation for the birth parent. Even if she moves and does not give a forwarding address, she may do so with great sadness, believing it is best for the child if she disappears. Most birth parents grieve for years over the placement, and always carry some sadness inside them because of it.

Essential

Counselors advise birth moms to write their children letters explaining why they gave them up, to go into detail about doing what was right and expressing that they loved them enough to let them go. If you receive such a letter when you adopt, keep it for your child to read when he is older.

Even with the prevalence of open adoptions today, many birth moms do decide against them. Most women who choose closed adoptions do so because they want to move on with their lives.

Birth parents who are forced to relinquish their rights to the state (or, in some international adoptions, who place a child because they have no real choice between watching the child starve or placing her) also suffer loss and must grieve. A parent who made bad decisions may turn his or her life around and suffer a lot of regret about the termination.

Before you or your child begins to search for a birth parent, it is important that you understand the choices and process the birth parents went through in making the choice, or dealing with the situation if an overt or conscious choice was not an option.

When to Search

If you and your child are in an open adoption, most of her questions may have been answered as she grew up. If the adoption was semi-open or closed to a certain degree, questions may be more difficult to answer.

Deciding when to search for a birth parent will depend on your child's age, your situation, and the way the adoption was handled. Most professionals advise that searches not be started during a crisis, such as immediately after the death of an adoptive parent or an angry, explosive episode.

Curiosity

Whether you adopted your child as a newborn or toddler or she didn't come home to you until she'd endured years in an institution, she will have questions and be curious about her birth family. Curiosity is normal, and does not mean you should drop everything and hire a private investigator tomorrow.

Most of the time, curiosity is best dealt with as it comes up, by answering the questions with the information you do have. It will first surface when she begins to understand biological relationships, at about age seven or eight. If you are uncomfortable with questions and curiosity about the birth family, your feelings will be noticed by your child, whether or not you actually say anything.

Don't think that she has forgotten if the questions stop. The most likely reason for her to stop asking questions is her recognition of your uncomfortable feelings on the subject and an unwillingness to hurt you.

Alert!

If your child was abandoned or removed from his birth family for reasons of abuse, neglect, or criminal activity, you may be forbidden by law from searching for his birth parents while he's under eighteen or twenty-one years old (this varies by state).

By the time your child enters adolescence, you can be sure she has already thought about her adoptive status and biological family. Those thoughts will be mixed up with the normal pulling away that adolescents do to begin to establish their identities as independent adults.

Support the Search

Because your child might be hesitant to mention curiosity or feelings about her biological origins, you should reassure her that you understand and support her. Adoptees generally have much more satisfactory and warm relationships with parents who have been honest about their adoptions and who validate their feelings and support them at the proper time in searching.

 Essential

If you adopted through foster care, it is likely the parents' rights were terminated and direct contact is forbidden during childhood. However, some child welfare agencies will serve as an intermediate contact between adoptive and biological parents if a request is made to support the emotional needs of your child. This is most typically done with a therapist's involvement.

Appropriate Age for Searching

The proper time to search for birth parents isn't the same for every child. The time will depend on the circumstances of her birth, the openness of the adoption, and the specifics of your relationship. Many experts advise parents to share the information they have with their child and then let her know that when she is an adult, she is free to locate her birth parents. Other experts believe it is appropriate to assist a teen in her search.

If your child is younger than four or five, you should wait a few years before talking about actively searching. At this point, your child isn't mature enough to understand enough to ask you to search. You should still answer questions that come up and gather or protect important information that will be useful when the time to search comes. This information should include copies of your adoption decree, her original birth certificate (if you can get it), and names and addresses of any biological relatives.

An especially vulnerable time is the mid-teens. At this age, your child may really need to find her birth parents. If your child is fourteen or fifteen and in a closed adoption, but you know her family name, you can initiate some searching, such as looking in the phone book or talking to your agency. Do this with your child and demonstrate that you are secure in the fact that you are her real family and that you understand and validate her feelings.

 **Fact**

> The National Council for Adoption (NCFA), a leading adoption group, states, "Birth parents and adult adopted persons who desire to have contact should be able to do so, when both agree. Otherwise, both should be able to control the release of their identifying information and whether and when contacts are to occur."

If you do find your child's birth family when she's a teen, your family dynamics will become even more challenging than usual. If your child decides she'd rather live with her birth mom or dad, do not allow it, just as you wouldn't allow any other life-altering choice made by a minor child.

Most adoptees are in their late twenties or early thirties when they begin searching. They are generally female, middle class, and married. More than half of all searchers are looking for siblings or extended family members. Some adoptees never search or don't start until their fifties or sixties. When the search is delayed until late in life, it rarely results in reunion with birth parents, but it can result in a satisfying relationship with siblings and cousins.

Searching

If you will be searching for your child's birth parents, the method you use will hinge on how much information is available and how much money you wish to spend. Remember that searching is essentially your child's prerogative, once he becomes an adult, but your relationship while he grows up will determine whether his search is underground or out in the open. You can greatly reinforce his attachment by taking your cues from him and being supportive. Your support can be in the form of hiring a service or private detective or finding resources.

Before You Begin

You or your child may be anxious to hit the ground running for the search, but there are steps you should take before you undertake a search. Before beginning a search, do the following:

- **Gather all documentation,** such as adoption petition and consent papers, court orders, birth certificates, travel information, and anything else that has been saved from the adoption.
- **Write down information you or anyone else involved might remember,** such as where the birth mother lived, or that the birth father was a student at a certain college, or the name of the social worker involved.
- **Contact the state or agency that handled the adoption and ask for any information they can offer you.** This will most likely be information that does not directly identify the birth parents, but there may be important clues.
- **If you don't know the name of the agency,** contact your state department of vital records for the state the child was born in and they can provide that information.

Putting together this basic information up front can make it a lot easier to locate the birth parent.

Investing the time and energy in his search is cathartic for your child. He may feel overwhelmed and frustrated at times as he encounters dead ends, but he's exercising control over a situation where he didn't have any as a child.

Online Searches

You or your child can do online searches yourself to try to locate birth parents. If you know the names, you can begin with basic searches for the name alone. If you have other details, such as a city, hospital, or other information, you can include that in your search. If your child was adopted through an agency, the agency may have a program that allows adoptees and birth parents to contact each other should each consent. There are also many, many message boards where adoptees and birth parents hoping to connect can post information and sometimes find each other. Reunion registries exist for every state and many agencies.

Alert!

If you are searching for a birth parent from an international adoption, you will likely have to hire a professional searcher who has contacts in the country and speaks the language.

Organizations that can help you and your child include the Council for Equal Rights in Adoption (CERA), which maintains an updated list of support groups around the country, and the International Soundex Reunion Registry (ISRR), *www.issr.net*, which is a free service for adoptees and birth families.

Hiring a Professional

You may wish to hire a confidential intermediary—a professional who works for the state who seeks out members of the adoption triad and brings them together if there is consent. You may also wish to consider hiring a private investigator, who does not need the consent of the birth parents to release information. It is very important that if you do hire someone, that you ask for references and do your homework to make sure this is a person or agency who has a successful track record in reunions. Searching for a birth parent is a very emotional journey, and there are too many people seeking to prey on that vulnerability.

Preparing Your Child for Contact

If your child is searching, you will need to help her prepare for the reality of the meeting, should it come. Whatever her history is, with all its ups and downs, it can be handled if she feels loved and understood. If you make contact while your child is a minor, have in mind boundaries and particulars that will protect your sense of family and your child's primary attachment.

Set Expectations

Before you or your child begins the search, talk about what her expectations are. Does she just want to meet her birth mother or is she hoping to be welcomed into the bosom of the family? Try to help her create some realistic expectations that are grounded in the possibilities of the situation.

Gently help your child understand that she may not be able to locate her birth family. If she does find them, there is the chance that they will not want to meet with her. This kind of rejection can be very painful for an adoptee who has waited her whole life for the chance to see her genetic roots.

If your child is successful in locating and meeting her birth parent, you should help her be prepared for the fact that there may not be that instant connection she is hoping for. She may physically resemble the person she finds, but they may be completely different and incompatible in all other ways. Don't let her get her hopes up too high, and suggest that she take things one step at a time. No matter what happens, you will be there to love her, listen to her, and support her, and she will always be an important part of your family. Finding the birth parent will not in any way end your bond or relieve you of your responsibility to her.

Initial Contact

Making the first call to a birth parent can be a nerve-wracking experience. If you are assisting your teen in a search, rehearse with her what she will say when she makes the call. Remind her that the birth parent she is contacting may not have told other people in her life about the baby she placed for adoption, so she should always ask if it is a good time to talk.

Suggest to your child that the parent being contacted will likely need some time to work through his or her emotions, and might not have the initial reaction that matches her expectations. Be sure that she remembers to exchange contact information before getting off the phone so that the parent can contact her in the future.

Setting Boundaries after Initial Contact

Once you or your child have located a birth parent, it can be hard to know where to start. Your first couple of meetings should happen on neutral territory when possible, such as a restaurant, park, or other public place. This is especially true if your child is younger, there are similar-aged children in the birth family, or there's a disparity in economic circumstances between your households. Depending on their ages, children can be jealous or angry about each other's toys, clothes, or possessions. If your child has significantly more material possessions, she may feel guilty and can be set up for emotional problems that will get in the way of building any sort of relationship.

If your child is still living at home, ongoing contact will depend on your assessment of the situation. You may decide to continue meeting. As comfort levels increase, and if circumstances allow, you may visit one another's homes. The key is to allow time for relationships to develop. You can't expect everyone to fall in love with each other all at once.

 Essential

Your relationship with your child's birth family may develop into something similar to that of in-laws or progress to the connection of cousins or other extended family. Continue to support your child in maintaining connections once the initial contacts are made, as long as your best instincts tell you the relationship is beneficial to her.

Your teenager may be excited about finding her birth parents, but after an initial meeting may settle back into her life with you, causing you to have to prompt her into sending e-mails or making phone calls. Be careful how you prompt, however, because having a relationship with her birth family is up to her, not you. Your responsibility is to facilitate rather than force.

There's a big difference between facilitating connection and extended family ties versus abdicating primary family roles. If you think the contact is creating serious issues and your child becomes defiant, distant, and rebellious, run—don't walk—to your adoption therapist and get counseling for you and the whole family. You would also be justified in cutting off contact if the birth family encourages your child to reject her adoptive family or has a very negative effect on your child.

Helping Your Child Deal with Rejection

If your child finds his biological mother, he may fantasize that he'll be welcomed with open arms. Unfortunately, that may not happen.

Some searches don't have a happy ending, and your child must be prepared to face that fact. For example, Annette's birth mother didn't want to be found and when Annette persevered, the woman told her in no uncertain terms that she had absolutely no interest in resurrecting that part of her life. She hadn't told her parents about her pregnancy, nor did her husband realize she'd given up a baby before he met her.

You and your child cannot control the actions and feelings of the other members of the adoption triad, but the act of searching will allow your child to feel empowered.

If your adoption was open and became closed because the birth family stopped contact and disappeared, your child's fantasies and feelings of rejection may be more problematic than if the adoption was closed from the beginning. You may need to consult with a therapist and go into family counseling.

You need to help your child understand that the birth parent is not rejecting him as a person, but is instead turning away from that part of his or her life. Some birth parents find it hard to move on with their lives if they maintain contact with their birth child. Try to help your child respect the birth parent's choice and remind him that he has a family that loves and accepts him completely.

 **Alert!**

When an open adoption fades away and you lose contact with your child's birth family, continue to collect pictures and information about your child—perhaps sending it to your agency or adoption professional. At some point, your child will likely embark on a search and will need concrete proof that you weren't the one to stonewall his connection to his heritage.

When to Give Up

Coming to grips with the facts that her birth family cannot be found will be difficult for your child, no matter what her age. This situation is most common in international adoptions or when a child has been abandoned.

If your child is young or still lives at home, you have more control over when to stop searching. No matter what your child's age, you should affirm your child's reality and weep with her about not having enough information, or about the choices of adults beyond your sphere of control. Put your arms around her, tell her you're sorry, and remind her of your love.

It is possible that your child could undertake another search at some point in the future. Several years ago it would have been inconceivable that the Internet would be such a huge tool in adoption searches—there could be new technology years from now that will offer more assistance. It's also possible that information about the birth parents could surface in a few years, such as through newspaper reports about them.

Your support and guidance during the process of searching will strengthen your relationship with your child. Most adoptive parents and adoptees report greater closeness and love for each other, no matter what the outcome of the search was.

CHAPTER 19

Helping Adopted Children Become Adults

If you're successful as a parent, your children will grow up and leave home as independent, self-reliant adults. If your child is very young, you might think you have a long time before you need to worry about such grown-up issues, but once your little one has progressed successfully through the first two stages of attachment, you should be looking to her future. To do so, you must help her grow to become a responsible, contributing adult. Your role as a parent never ends; it just changes as your child grows.

Shifting Your Role

When your child grows up and starts her own family, she will become responsible for herself, but you will still be her parent, and her children will be your grandsons and granddaughters. Your role in her adult life will be just as important as your role in her childhood, but it must take a different form.

It is common for adult adoptees to face issues of identity and loss at milestone moments in their lives, such as graduation, marriage, or having a child. Accept that your child will always deal with some lingering pain related to the adoption, and help her face the milestones in her life with joy and a feeling of pride.

When your child grows up and moves out of your home, respect her independence and her right to make choices about a career, relationships, and other areas of life. The fact that your child was adopted in no way impacts her right and ability to choose her own life course.

Special Needs Adult Children

Adopting a child with emotional or physical disabilities may necessitate open-ended parenting, parenting that doesn't stop at a certain age. If you are in this situation, be sensitive to what your child needs at various stages. As he grows up, you should shift your thinking to accommodate his reality. However, you can give him the autonomy of an adult by declaring him to be one and allowing him to make choices that don't interfere with his safety or health.

 Essential

If your child is mentally or emotionally disabled, you may need to live close enough to supervise her finances, because she can be victimized. Also, you may need to help her with activities such as shopping and meal planning.

Help your child qualify for Social Security, disability payments, Medicaid, and housing subsidies as appropriate. He may live happily in an assisted living or a group home, supported by your caring, watchful presence. Although he may never be able to live independently, his status as a loved member of your family will give him autonomy.

You will also want to talk with a financial planner to help you ensure your child will be financially stable should something happen to you. This may involve creating a trust. If he is legally incompetent, you need to line up who would become his guardian or conservator, should you no longer be present.

College

You and your child may be worried about what school she will get into and how your family will afford the cost of higher education. This is a time in your child's life when the adoption will have some payoffs and may offer her a few advantages other students cannot access.

Finances

As the parent of an adopted child, you have some avenues of assistance available to you that other parents do not. There are a wide variety of college scholarships and tuition waivers available for children who are adopted, who have spent time in foster care, or who were in an orphanage. Talk with your child's high school guidance counselor and Google the words "adoption scholarship" to find information.

Admissions

Depending on your child's circumstances, the adoption may be helpful in college admissions. Adoption itself is not so unusual these days, but a child who was adopted at an older age, spent time in foster care, or who lived in an orphanage for a time has special circumstances which may interest college admissions staff and present an advantage. Additionally, a child who is of a minority race, other nationality, or has special needs will also get attention because colleges strive to create diverse student bodies.

Combating the Effects of Adoption in Adult Life

Whether your child spent nearly all of his life in your home or a relatively short time, he will continue to deal with the adoption all of his adult life. If he has been unable to find his birth parents, that lack of knowledge may always bother him. If he was removed from an abusive home, he may have emotional issues he is still dealing with. Your role is to support him, love him, and take his feelings seriously, yet refuse to let him randomly play the adoption card for sympathy.

Focus on the Positive

Everybody's life includes lots of unfortunate experiences, but dwelling on negativity merely reinforces negative feelings and raises destructive chemicals in the brain. Conversely, focusing on positive feelings reinforces those feelings and produces endorphins that reduce blood pressure and promote tranquility. Recall the good times and silly things that have happened.

Reframe Traumatic Events

Frame painful or hurtful episodes as positively as possible for your child. You've probably been doing this for many years when it comes to the adoption. You can also do this about events that have happened in your own family. Instead of allowing your child to go off into the world feeling guilt or sorrow about them, reframe them so that you both understand and forgive what happened. If your child ran away from home, reframe this so that in retrospect it becomes an event that helped you understand each other more, rather than some awful mistake he made that hurt everyone.

Fear of Loss

Many children who have been adopted carry a fear of loss throughout their whole life. Even if your child was not old enough to remember the adoption, it is still a fact he has learned about and lived with. Some adult adoptees find it hard to develop close relationships because they harbor a fear that the person they love will eventually leave them, just as the birth parents did.

If you gave your child a loving, safe home, you have done your part. When he is an adult, it is up to him to find a way to work through these feelings if they are a problem. You can suggest a therapist, be available to talk, and reassure him of your love and support, but as an adult, he must take the reins and find his way through it.

Cement Family Bonds Through Traditions

Every family has its own rituals that reinforce unique bonds. The rituals can be as simple as eating pancakes every Sunday or as complex as dip-net fishing for King salmon in Alaska each summer. Traditions such as these help create bonds in adoptive families. The most enduring traditions cost little money, like the family who takes one evening a month to focus on one member, to describe in verse, drawing, or recording just why that person is special. Your family traditions will remain important as your child becomes an adult.

Shifting Traditions to Accommodate Growth

Your traditions may change as your child leaves your home. It may no longer be possible to have Sunday movie nights if your child has moved away. Your child might not arrive home for Christmas until that morning, meaning you will have to shift your Christmas Eve traditions to fit her schedule. Part of being a family is being flexible enough to change your traditions to encompass your child's growth.

Your child may also use her new independence as a way of testing whether she really is a part of the family. If you don't wait to grill the hot dogs on the Fourth of July until she gets there, she might wrongly interpret that to mean she really isn't a member of the family. Your role is to make sure she knows how important she is, but help her understand the entire family cannot revolve around her. Some traditions have to stick, and if she is late, that's okay.

Creating New Traditions

As your children grow, you may need to create new traditions to meet the growing family's needs. You could plan to meet at a seaside cottage for a week in the summer each year or create new ways to keep in touch when you are apart.

For example, one family writes a bimonthly newsletter for members who live all over the country. The responsibility of editor rotates yearly. The designated editor makes sure each sibling and the parents have a current address list, then sends out a request for articles, jokes, or comments.

Weddings

Seeing your child married is a special moment. The presence or absence of birth parents can take an already emotionally charged day and push it over the edge. The best way to handle things is to remind yourself that it is your child's day and you are there to help his dreams come true.

With Birth Parents

If birth parents are part of your child's life, your child may want them involved in the wedding. There is the potential for a lot of hurt feelings, however. Think about how you would feel if your child asked his birth mother to accompany you as you walk him down the aisle? How would you feel if the birth parents or extended birth family were in family photos?

 Essential

Your daughter- or son-in-law is a lot like an adopted child. He came from elsewhere and has now become an integral part of your family. If you are able to welcome him as a child of your heart, just as you did with your adopted child, you are sure to have a wonderful, loving relationship with each other.

There are no set rules for how to handle the situation. Your child needs to do what feels right to him; your job is to support him, smile and remember it is his day, not yours. If you feel very strongly about some things, it is okay to express your feelings, but remember you can't make the decisions.

Without Birth Parents

If your child is not in contact with or has never been able to find his birth parents, his wedding can be a bittersweet day. He may be sad they are not there, and he may be angry that he cannot share this moment with them. Your child is an adult, and must cope with this situation in whatever way is best for him. You can offer support, a shoulder to cry on, and your undying love.

Grandchildren

Relationships with your grandchildren are different from your relationship with their parent (your child). Like parenting, grandparenting takes on different dimensions as the child grows up, and as the number of grandchildren increases.

Biological Grandchildren

If your child creates your grandchild biologically and you were never pregnant, you might think you don't have much to offer as your daughter or daughter-in-law goes through pregnancy and birth. The truth is, she can get all the medical information she needs from her health care provider; your support and love as she goes through the process is what she really needs.

If you adopted your child after infancy, you might feel a little bit at a loss when it comes to dealing with newborns. If you want to, you can take a baby-care class at your local hospital or read some books about newborns and babies. You and your child and her spouse are in the unique position of learning to care for a baby together. You'll all make mistakes, but a child who is raised in a loving home will reap the benefits. The process of pregnancy and birth will likely bring you and your child even closer.

Adopted Grandchildren

If your child chooses to adopt a child, you will be a font of information for her. You can offer advice and information about the process, the emotions, the challenges, and all the joy it brings. If your child is choosing adoption after infertility or loss, you may be able to share your own experiences if you went through the same thing.

Question?

How can I be sure I start my grandparenting the right way?
If you've been asked to help out, your responsibilities will be more along the lines of washing dishes, vacuuming, and cooking, rather than actually holding the baby. Babies must attach to their mommies and daddies first, then come grandmas and grandpas. Wait your turn!

Since you will be an old hand at adoption, your child will not have to face some of the hurdles that you might have dealt with, such as extended family members who are not completely on board with adoption.

A Final Word on Relating to Adult Children

Shifting your relationship to mentor and friend with your adult child and bonding with your grandchildren requires time and energy—both of which might be limited in your life. But spending that time and energy, and sacrificing to stay connected, will reap great rewards.

You will become the Keeper of Family, the person who connects your own parents and grandparents with younger generations. Family is all about love, devotion, and time to forge the ties that bind you together as the years pass.

APPENDIX A

Additional Resources

Adoption Factbook IV. National Council for Adoption. (Sterling, VA: PMR Printing Company, Inc., 2007). This large resource book covers adoption statistics, domestic adoption, adoption and foster care, international adoption, the adoption process, and a detailed discussion of mutual consent and openness in adoption.

Adoptive Families Magazine: This magazine provides adoptive families with up-to-the-minute information about finding and raising children from all over the world and of all ages.
39 West 37th Street, 15th Floor
New York, NY 10018
646-366-0830
www.adoptivefamilies.com

Adesman, Andrew, M.D. *Parenting Your Adopted Child: A Positive Approach to Building a Strong Family.* (New York: McGraw-Hill, 2004). Balanced and authoritative treatment of all types of adoption, especially excellent in discussion of transracial adoptions.

Berlin, Peter R., and Jerry Stone. *A Personal Touch On . . . Adoption: Support Group in a Book.* (Los Angeles, CA: A Personal Touch Publishing, 2005). Numerous personal stories from birth mothers, adoptees, and adoptive parents who adopted across racial lines or were in nontraditional families.

Curtis, Jamie Lee. *Tell Me Again about the Night I Was Born.* (New York: Harper Collins Publishers, 1996). Beautifully illustrated (by Laura Cornell) and sweetly told story of a child adopted at birth; excellent for reading to young children.

Davenport, Dawn. *The Complete Book of International Adoption.* (New York: Random House, 2006). Ms. Davenport hosts the Internet radio show, "Creating a Family: Talk about Adoption and Infertility." *www.findingyourchild.com*

Dobson, James. *Parenting Isn't for Cowards*. (Waco, TX: Word, 1987). A readable, kind, and hopeful guide for parents of children from infancy through adolescence. More than twenty years after publication, Dr. Dobson's advice is still practical and on target.

Doss, Helen. *The Family Nobody Wanted*. (Boston: Little, Brown and Company, 1954). Wonderful story of Helen and Carl Doss, who adopted ten children, many of whom were biracial or handicapped.

Eldridge, Sherrie, *Twenty Things Adopted Kids Wish Their Adoptive Parents Knew*. (New York: Dell, 1999). Personal account and ideas about the adoption experience; excellent for giving the viewpoint of an adult who was adopted as a child.

Eyre, Richard, and Linda Eyre. *Empty-Nest Parenting*. (Salt Lake City, UT: Deseret Book Company, 2002). A calm and wise guide for parents who reach the end of their legal responsibility for their children, but want to maintain love and connection and support adult children as they launch their independent lives.

Fackrell, Tamara. *The Potentially Sane Mother's Guide to Raising Young Children*. (Salt Lake City, UT: Deseret Book, 2005). Inspiration and comfort for parents of small children, with specific tips on building trust and accountability while enjoying the adventure of parenting.

Featherstone, Helen. *A Difference in the Family: Life with a Disabled Child*. (New York: Basic Books, 1980). Excellent discussion of strategies for helping siblings attach and families thrive. Also, gives insights into how disabled people feel about and deal with their surroundings.

Fodor, Margie Druss. *Megan's Law: Protection of Privacy*. (Berkeley Heights, NJ: Enslow Publishers, 2001). Young-adult level of discussion about legal and privacy issues surrounding convicted sex offenders; considers unintended consequences and problems with using DNA registries.

Foli, Karen J., Ph.D., and John R. Thompson, M.D. *The Post-Adoption Blues: Overcoming the Unforeseen Challenges of Adoption.* (New York: Rodale Press, 2004). Highly recommended! This readable book gives hope and ideas to adoptive parents who wonder why the experience they most coveted isn't turning out the way they thought it would.

Garner, Abigail. *Families Like Mine: Children of Gay Parents Tell It Like It Is.* (New York: HarperCollins, 2004). The author, the child of a gay father, researched the stories of more than fifty children of gays or lesbians who are now adults. A valuable book for those who want to understand the "gifts and challenges of being raised in families that are often labeled 'controversial.'"

Gray, Deborah. *Attaching in Adoption.* (Indianapolis, IN: Perspectives Press, 2002). An indispensable and well-written guide for parents dealing with attachment issues of children from abusive or neglected backgrounds.

Hopkins-Best, Mary. *Toddler Adoption: The Weaver's Craft.* (Indianapolis, IN: Perspectives Press, 1997). Readable, reassuring book about special issues in adopting toddlers. Gives specific, helpful advice for addressing attachment and cultural challenges.

Johnston, Patricia Irwin. *Adoption Is a Family Affair!* (Perspectives Press, 2001). This book focuses on extended family members' points of view and gives advice for building close relationships. It's filled with information and advice based on interviews and experiences of thousands of adoptive families, and it contains excellent resources.

Jones, Sandy. *Comforting Your Crying Baby.* (New York: Innova Publishing, 1992). Kind and compassionate advice for parents from first timers to those who care for foster babies or who may have multiple children. Discusses the reasons babies cry and building communication and family attachment.

Latham, Glenn I., Ph.D. *The Power of Positive Parenting.* (North Logan, UT: P & T Inc., 2003). Workbook-style manual for addressing all aspects of applying behavioral principles at home and being the in-charge but loving adult.

Lev, Arlene Istar, CSW. *The Complete Lesbian and Gay Parenting Guide.* (New York: Berkley, 2004). An interesting book written by a lesbian adoptive parent that gives specific suggestions and details pertaining to forming "alternative" families, understanding legal methods for protecting particular lifestyles, and the realities of adoptive parenting.

Libal, Joyce, in consultation with Lisa Albers, M.D.; Carolyn Bridgemohan, M.D.; Laurie J. Glader, M.D.; Cindy Croft, M.A. *Somebody Hear Me Crying: Youth in Protective Services.* (Broomall, PA: Mason Crest Publishers, 2004). Read for help with understanding risks and identifying behaviors of abused and or neglected children.

Liptak, Karen. *Adoption Controversies.* (New York: Franklin Watts, 1993). Discusses the impact of adoption on the adoption triad: the child, the adoptive parents, and the birth parents. Short essays give pros and cons of different forms of adoption from surrogacy to transracial adoptions.

MacLeod, Jean, and Sheena Macrae, Ph.D. *Adoption Parenting: Creating a Toolbox, Building Connections.* (Warren, NJ: EMK Press, 2006). Essays and articles by adoptive parents and adoption professionals that cover everything from understanding the unique issues surrounding adoption to specific techniques for dealing with disciplining an abused child, developing family bonds, and transitioning through childhood stages into adulthood.

McLean, Michael. *From God's Arms to My Arms to Yours.* (Salt Lake City, UT: Shadow Mountain Press, 2007). This is a small, hardcover keepsake book with beautiful pictures and short, touching essays, plus a CD with original songs about all aspects of adoption—a birth mother's choice, adoptive families' yearnings, adoptee perspectives, etc.

Melina, Lois Ruskai, and Sharon Kaplan Roszia. *The Open Adoption Experience*. (New York: Harper Collins Publishers, 1993). Early writing on open adoptions; includes many excellent references and resources.

Melina, Lois Ruskai. *Raising Adopted Children: Practical, Reassuring Advice for Every Adoptive Parent*. (New York: Harper Collins Publishers, 1998). Excellent advice for helping children attach to their adoptive parents, and an early reference for dealing with birth families.

Meyer, Donald J., Patricia F. Vadasy, and Rebecca R. Fewell. *Living with a Brother or Sister with Special Needs: A Book for Sibs*. (Seattle: University of Washington Press, 1985). Young-adult level of information for siblings who live with a disabled person. Compilation of lectures, essays, and articles that help kids understand causes of different disabilities and how to cope with embarrassment.

Muzi, Malina Jo. *Your Kids: Their Lives*. (Merion Station, PA: Pink Roses Publishing, 2006). Essays and observations about all aspects of parenting, from infancy through adolescence and young adulthood; contains excellent advice about connecting with and guiding children without force or neglect.

Paton, Jean M. *The Adopted Break Silence: The Experiences and Views of Forty Adults Who Were Once Adopted Children*. (Philadelphia, PA: Life History Study Center, 1954). Early writings describing the pain of adults who had no information about their biological families.

Player, Corrie Lynne, M.Ed. *Loving Firmness: Successfully Raising Teenagers Without Losing Your Mind*. (Denver, CO: Mapletree Publishing Company, 2006). Practical, readable, and inspiring information for parents of teens.

Purvis, Karyn B., Ph.D., David R. Cross, Ph.D., and Wendy Lyons Sunshine. *The Connected Child: Bring Hope and Healing to Your Adoptive Family*. (New York: McGraw Hill, 2007). Extremely practical advice for parents who adopt children from other countries or cultures with troubled backgrounds and or special behavioral or emotional needs.

Reef, Catherine. *Alone in the World: Orphans and Orphanages in America.* (New York: Houghton Mifflin Co., 2005). Readable, well-written discussion of reasons for orphanages and why they're no longer part of the child welfare system in the United States.

Russell, Marlou, Ph.D. *Adoption Wisdom: A Guide to the Issues and Feelings of Adoption.* (Broken Branch Productions, 2000) Dr. Russell has spent a lifetime gathering information about the adoption experience. Her work enables adoptive parents to understand the feelings and issues of the children they welcome.

Schlessinger, Laura, Ph.D. *Bad Childhood Good Life.* (New York: HarperCollins Publishers, 2006). Dr. Laura describes how adults can put aside the crippling effects of an abusive childhood and take control of their lives. Most of her advice is also helpful for adoptive parents who bring children into their homes from dysfunctional families.

Schlessinger, Laura, Ph.D. *Stupid Things Parents Do to Mess Up Their Kids.* (New York: Quill, an imprint of HarperCollins, 2002). Specific, honest, sometimes disturbing advice about asserting and maintaining parental authority that changes as a child grows toward independence.

Seligman, Martin E. Ph.D., Karen Reivich, M.A., Lisa Jaycox, Ph.D., and Jane Gillham, Ph.D. *The Optimistic Child.* (New York: Houghton Mifflin Company, 1995). Clear, sometimes complicated, instructions about "inoculating" children against depression through specific parenting techniques.

Sember, Brette McWhorter. *The Adoption Answer Book: Your Complete Guide to a Successful Adoption.* (Naperville, IL: Sphinx Publishing, An Imprint of Sourcebooks, Inc., 2007). Excellent legal resource for those contemplating adoption; gives specifics about open adoption, home studies, surrogacy, etc. Has extensive appendices with up-to-date references.

Sember, Brette McWhorter. *Gay & Lesbian Parenting Choices: From Adopting or Using a Surrogate to Choosing the Perfect Father.* (Franklin

Lakes, NJ: Career Press, 2006). A comprehensive look at the options available to same-sex couples wanting to start a family. The author, a former attorney, provides information on international, domestic and state agency, private, and facilitator-led adoption.

Simon, Rita J., and Howard Altstein. *Adoption Across Borders (a 30-Year Study of Transracial and Intercountry Adoptions)*. (Lanham, MD: Roman & Littlefield Publishers, Inc., 2000). An essential resource for parents who adopt outside their ethnic group or internationally; gives research-based information, not anecdotal or emotional.

Snow, Judith E. *How It Feels to Have a Gay or Lesbian Parent: A Book by Kids for Kids of All Ages*. (Binghampton, NY: Hawthorn Press, 2004). A collection of stories from twenty-eight children, ranging in age from seven to twenty-eight years. This book has validity for children currently being raised by gay or lesbian parents and is a useful tool for therapists and educators in family and multicultural counseling.

Sonna, Linda, Ph.D. *The Everything® Parent's Guide to Children with ADD/ADHD*. (Avon, MA: Adams Media, 2005). Readable, easy-to-access information for all parents of ADD- and ADHD-diagnosed (or suspected) children.

Sonna, Linda, Ph.D. *The Everything® Parent's Guide to Raising Siblings*. (Avon, MA: Adams Media, 2006). Dr. Sonna gives wise, warm, and accessible advice to parents about all sorts of sibling issues, including adopted siblings and maintaining relationships with siblings who don't live with the child.

St. Clair, Brita. *99 Ways to Drive Your Child Sane*. (Glenwood Springs, CO: Families by Design Publishers, 1999). Fun, helpful little book that gives overstressed parents of children with serious emotional problems tools and tips to cope with situations most parents wouldn't even consider.

Taylor, Rebecca M., MSW. "Why Adoption," *Ensign Magazine*, January 2008, pp. 47–52.

Verrier, Nancy. *The Primal Wound: Understanding the Adopted Child.* (Lafayette, CA: Nancy Verrier, 2007). One of the earliest books to address differences between biological and adopted children. Well-written and engaging style.

Walsh, David, Ph.D. *No: Why Kids of All Ages Need to Hear It and Ways Parents Can Say It.* (New York: Free Press, 2007). Very well-written, helpful, and kind parenting tool.

Walsh, David, Ph.D. *Why Do They Act That Way? A Survival Guide to the Adolescent Brain for You and Your Teen.* (New York: Free Press, 2004). Dr. Walsh's book is one of the most readable and important books about teenagers ever published.

Warren, Andrea. *Orphan Train Rider: One Boy's True Story.* (New York: Houghton Mifflin Company, 1996). Young-adult-level description of the orphan trains that operated in the United States from 1854 to 1930, where children were sent from large cities to homes in the Midwest and far west.

Williams, Mary E., *Opposing Viewpoints: Adoption.* (Farmington Hills, MI: Greenhaven Press, Imprint of Thomson Gale, a part of The Thomson Corporation, 2006). Interesting and useful collection of essays about all sides of the adoption issue.

Young, Curtis. "The Missing Piece: Adoption Counseling in Pregnancy Resource Centers," *Heartlink*, January 2001. Discussion of importance of semi-open adoptions as a way for birth parents to reconcile their decision to relinquish.

Organizations, Professionals, and Helpful Web Sites

Adoption.org

This Web site is devoted to helping adult adoptees search and biological families find each other. For more information, contact Tina Musso
9822 Highland Creek
San Antonio, TX 78245
tmusso@usa.net
www.adoption.org

Adoption Alliance, Inc.

This agency is located in Colorado and offers a wide range of adoption services, including education and support groups for postadoption counseling.
www.adoptall.com

Adoption ARK

This agency is licensed in Illinois, California, and Texas. They specialize in international adoptions and also have a humanitarian and fundraising division to support orphanages and children not available for adoption.
www.specialadoption.com

Adoption Registry Connect

A place for adoptees and birth parents to connect.
www.adopteeconnect.com

Adoption Resource Center

This agency specializes in placing children of color.
4701 Pine Street, J-7
Philadelphia, PA 19143
215-748-1441
www.adoptionarc.com

AdoptUSKids

This photo listing of eligible U.S. children is a service of the Adoption Exchange Association.
8015 Corporate Drive, Suite C
Baltimore, MD 21236
888-200-4005
www.adoptuskids.org

American Adoption Congress

This organization's mission statement is "We promote honesty, openness and respect for family connections in adoption, foster care and assisted reproduction."
Lynne Banks, Regional Director
lbanks8928@sio.midco.net
www.americanadoptioncongress.org

CAP Learning Associates, Inc Workshop, "The Teenage Brain: An Engine Without a Driver"

Research into how teen brains differ from adult brains and the special considerations parents must keep in mind to help their adolescents avoid or minimize risky behavior.
Lee B. Daniel, Director, *ldaniel@numail.org*

Center for Adoption Support and Education (C.A.S.E.)

This is an active organization with a varied, helpful program.
4000 Blackburn Lane, Suite 260
Burtonsville, MD 20866
www.adoptionsupport.org

Child Welfare Information Gateway

See National Child Welfare Resource Center for Adoption.
www.childwelfare.gov

Child Welfare League of America (Making Children a National Priority)

The CWLA is one of the oldest groups to address child welfare issues. They're a great organization for adoptive parents and professionals and serve as a clearinghouse for dozens of organizations.
440 First Street NW, Third Floor
Washington, DC 20001-2085
202-638-2952
www.cwla.org

Comeunity

Adoption information and support.
www.comeunity.com

Dave Thomas Foundation for Adoption

This organization is devoted to finding permanency for all adoptable children in foster care.
4150 Tuller Road, Suite 204
Dublin, OH 43017
www.davethomasfoundationforadoption.org

Families By Design

Nancy Thomas organized this group to provide education and support to adoptive families and children with attachment issues.
P.O. Box 2812
Glenwood Spring, CO 81602
970-524-4111
www.attachment.org

Gay.com
This site includes articles and information on same-sex couple adoption and family issues.
www.gay.com/families

Generations United

GU sponsors education and legislation designed to help kinship adoptions take place and flourish.
Donna Butts, Executive Director
2005 Market Street, Suite 1700
Philadelphia, PA 19103-7077
215-575-9050
www.gu.org

Grandparents As Parents

This approachable, excellent organization "provides programs and services to meet the urgent and ongoing needs of grandparents and other relative caregivers raising at risk children."
Madelyn Gordon, Executive Director
madelyn@grandparentsasparents.org
818-264 0880
www.grandparentsasparents.org

Great Kids, Inc.

A large organization with professional-level training courses for social and mental health care workers, as well as curriculum to support all phases of child development.
Betsy Dew
626-345-0684
www.greatkidsinc.org

Impact Publications, Inc.

Impact Publications targets foster parents, as well as adoptive parents who adopt from the foster care system.
www.impact-publications.com

Intercountry Adoption

State Department Web site offering information on how the State Department can assist with international adoption.
http://travel.state.gov/family/adoption/adoption_485.html

Lambda Legal

"Lambda Legal is the oldest national organization pursuing high-impact litigation, public education and advocacy on behalf of equality and civil rights for lesbians, gay men, bisexuals, transgender people and people with HIV." This includes adoption issues.
120 Wall Street, Suite 1500
New York, NY 10005
212-809-8585
www.lambdalegal.org

Lifeline Children and Family Services

This religious-based organization provides home studies, training, education, and support for licensing foster parents.
5301 W. Hwy 31
Corsicana, TX 75110
900 N. Beltline
Irving, TX 75060
972-514-0400
www.lifelinecfs.org

Life Site News

An online magazine that focuses on family values and cultural issues. Includes links to educational sites for parents and adoptive families.
www.lifesitenews.com

National Child Welfare Resource Center for Adoption

Adoption and post-legal-adoption services program planning, policy, and practice.
Natalie Lyons, LMSW, VP and Director
16250 Northland Drive, Ste. 120
Southfield, MI 48075
248-443-7080
www.ncradoption.org

National Clearinghouse on Child Abuse and Neglect Information

National Adoption Information Clearinghouse, "Gay and Lesbian Adoptive Parents: Resources for Professionals and Parents"
Fact sheet addressing issues faced by social workers evaluating same-sex couples for adoption and same-sex couples looking into adoption.
www.childwelfare.gov/pubs/f_gay/f_gay.pdf

National Council for Adoption (NCFA)

NCFA is a leading national organization that sponsors education and support for adoptive families and all members of the triad.
Tom Atwood, President and CEO
225 N. Washington Street
Alexandria, VA 22314
703-299-6633
tatwood@adoptioncouncil.org
www.adoptioncouncil.org

National Foster Parent Association

This group offers varied, in-depth trainings during state and regional meetings around the country and annually at locations that alternate across regions.
800-557-5238
www.NFPAinc.org

North American Council on Adoptable Children

This group specializes in helping to place special needs children, including sibling groups, and in providing ongoing support after placement.
970 Raymond Avenue, Suite 106
St. Paul, MN 55114-1149
651-644-3036
info@nacac.org
www.nacac.org

Pact: An Adoption Alliance

This caring, balanced group began nearly a decade ago to meet the needs of parents adopting across ethnic lines, especially those adopting racially mixed or African American children. They offer a full range of education, pre- and postadoption counseling, as well as publications and family camps.
Beth Hall, Director
4179 Piedmont Avenue, Suite 330
Oakland, CA 94611
800-243-9460
www.pactadopt.org

Russell, Marlou Ph.D., Clinical Psychologist/MFT

This psychologist works with children of all ages and their families, specializing in adoption issues. She offers education, information, and counseling for the lifelong impact of adoption.
1452 26th Street, Suite 103
Santa Monica CA 90404
310-829-1438
marlourussell@hotmail.com
www.marlourussellphd.com

Texas Christian Institute of Child Development

Director Karyn B. Purvis, Ph.D., and her staff at TCU have been pioneers in solving complex attachment problems for children adopted from orphanages, out of foster care, or who have emotional disorders stemming from illness, accident, or abuse.
TCU
Box 298920
Fort Worth, TX 76129
817-257-7681
www.child.tcu.edu

Tree House Foundation

Foster care support
www.treehousecommunities.org

United for Families, Inc.

This organization provides recruitment, training, and retention services for foster care, under contract from the state of Florida's Department of Children and Families.
Christine W. Demetriades
10570 S. Federal Highway, Suite 300
Port St. Lucie, Florida 34952
772-398-2920
christine.demetriades@UFF.US
www.uff.us

We Care: Child & Family Services

This is a private foster-parent recruitment, training, and support group that is licensed by the state of Kentucky.
125 West Park Street
P.O. Box 472
Guthrie, KY 42234
866-307-0401
www.wecarefamilies.com

Index

Same-sex couple adoption, 26
School, 143-45, 157-58, 171-
    72, 206-07, 242-43, 265
Self-harm, 246-48
Sexual abuse, 244-46
Sibling. *See also* Existing children
    adoption, 17-20
    bonds, 233-36
    groups, 39, 190-91
    rivalry, 234-35
Single parent adoption, 22-24
Special needs adoption, 38, 163-78
    dealing with, 169
    and education, 171-72
    and emotional disorders, 169-71
    and grief, 164-65
    and intellectual and emotional
        challenges, 175-76
    preparation, 166-68
    realities, 163-66
    support, 176-78
    and your emotions, 172-73
    and your family, 173-75
Stepparent adoption, 20-22
    and contact with biological
        family, 21
    emotional ramifications, 21-22
Support, 97-99, 176-78, 232-33

Toddlers, 103, 104-5, 110-14
Transracial adoption, 53-64
    attitudes and pressure
        from relatives, 57-58
    claiming rituals, 61-62
    culture for child
        development, 54-55
    developing your child's
        social skills, 62-64
    differences, 60
    good news about, 55-56
    heritage, 59
    race versus culture, 53-54
    strategies for parenting, 58-61
    your motives, 56-57
Tween and teen adoption,
    37-38, 147-61
    bonding, 154-56
    independence preparation,
        156-59
    peer pressure, 159-60
    preparation, 147-51
    recordkeeping, 160-61
    unique challenges of, 152-53